Black in white
*Caribbean children in the
United Kingdom*

by
Jean Harris Hendriks
and
John J. Figueroa

PITMAN PUBLISHING
128 Long Acre, London WC2E 9AN

A Division of Pearson Professional Limited

First published in Great Britain 1995

© Pearson Professional Limited 1995

British Library Cataloguing in Publication Data
A CIP catalogue record for this book can be obtained from the British Library.

ISBN 0 273 61671 4

10 9 8 7 6 5 4 3 2 1

Phototypeset by Northern Phototypesetting Co Ltd, Bolton
Printed and bound in Great Britain by Bell and Bain Ltd, Glasgow

The Publishers' policy is to use paper manufactured from sustainable forests.

To our daughters and sons

Contents

About the authors

Jean Harris Hendriks is a consultant in child and adolescent psychiatry, currently working in an English shire county and as an honorary consultant and senior lecturer at The Royal Free Hospital, London. During the 1950s she read medicine at the University of Birmingham at a time when many citizens of the Caribbean came to what they regarded as the mother country. Subsequently she worked in the East End of London, longstanding resting place and starting point for immigrants, and in towns with large Caribbean and Asian populations. She has a special interest in adoption and fostering and in the law as it affects children (*When Father Kills Mother*, Black, Wolkind and Harris Hendriks 1991). She continues her study of the effects of extreme family violence on children (*Child Psychiatry and the Law*, Harris Hendriks, Black and Kaplan 1993). This has led to a wider consideration of the effects upon children of trauma, grief and dislocation, issues highly relevant to immigration and the disruption of family relationships.

John J. Figueroa was born in Jamaica. He has taught in the USA, UK and Africa and in 1959 was the first native West Indian to be appointed to the post of Professor of Education and subsequently Dean at the University of the West Indies. He is currently Fellow at the Centre for Caribbean Studies at the University of Warwick.

His poetry appears in many anthologies and he has taught and lectured widely on Caribbean and African literature. He speaks English, Jamaican Creole, Spanish, Latin, a little French and less good Greek. Recent work includes *The Chase* (Collected Poetry 1941–1989) (1992) and a critical study of the poetry of Derek Walcott. He has edited several anthologies of Caribbean writing and a study of education in the Caribbean: *Society, Schools and Progress in the West Indies* (1971).

Acknowledgements

We are most grateful to Dorothy Figueroa for advice and critical comments, and to Diana Hendriks both for her advice and for the dedicated hard work involved in preparation of the manuscript.

Poem by John Figueroa, 'I have a Dream' by permission of the author.

Poem by Alan Harris, 'Being English' by permission of Jean Harris Hendriks on behalf of the author's estate.

Poems by A. L. Hendriks, 'Deeper than Blood', 'Mare Nostrum', 'Madonna of the Unknown Nation' and 'Their Mouths but not Their Hearts' by permission of Diana Hendriks on behalf of the author's estate.

Poem by Louise Bennett, 'Back to Africa' by kind permission of the author.

The poems 'Surviving' by Maureen Ismay and 'Dictionary Black' by Sista Roots reprinted on p. 7 and p. 94 are from *Watchers and Seekers: Creative Writing by Black Women in Britain* edited by Merle Collins and Rhonda Cobham, first published by The Women's Press Ltd, (1987), 34 Great Sutton Street, London EC1V 0DX.

Poem by Mervyn Morris, 'Case History, Jamaica' by kind permission of New Beacon Books Ltd, 76 Stroud Green Road, London N4 3EN.

Poem by Frank Collymore from *Caribbean Voices* by kind permission of Miss Ellice Collymore.

Extracts of a letter to Directors of Social Services from W. B. Utting by kind permission of the Controller of Her Majesty's Stationery Office.

Confidentiality

Stories illustrate common scenes and experiences and are compiled, identifying features having been changed or disguised, so as to illustrate the experiences of Caribbean children and their families in the UK without invading the privacy of individuals.

Introduction

An week by week dem shippin off
Dem countrymen like fire, fe immigrate an populate
De seat o' de Empire.

(Louise Bennett: Colonisation in reverse)

Caribbean citizens have been migrating since the late nineteenth century, in particular to Central America and the USA. They come from a region which stretches from the Bahamas in the north to Belize in Central America and Guyana in South America, a distance of about 1,500 miles. East to west the range is from Barbados to the Central American coast. The Caribbean Sea holds many islands of which the largest are the Dominican Republic and Haiti (one island known as Hispaniola), Cuba and Jamaica; the others are Puerto Rico, the Virgin Islands, the Leeward Islands, the Windward Islands, Barbados, and Trinidad and Tobago. Guyana and Belize in mainland Central and South America also contribute to the variety of cultures in the West Indies.

But Mustique to Bequia
You need a boat or plane
Swimming is for sharks, jelly fish and tourists.
Choose the bridge you fancy
The Caribbean drowns the dream.

(From Mare Nostrum by A.L. Hendriks)

The original population discovered by Columbus in 1492 were the Arawaks and the Caribs. Cruelty, overwork and disease removed them and for three hundred years the Spaniards were in charge. Later influences were English, Dutch and French.

Substantial numbers of the ancestors of the current inhabitants of the Caribbean were imported from Africa from the fifteenth to the middle of the seventeenth century. They worked on plantations and marriage between slaves was forbidden without the consent of their owner. Promiscuity was encouraged as a means of increasing the slave population and the property of the owner. Fathers had no possibility of fulfilling rights or duties towards their children.

As the British Empire spread, and Spanish power faded, Britain became known as the mother country to much of the Caribbean. Citizens speaking many different creole languages, based on English, Spanish, French or Dutch, and of many origins, lived together in variable harmony.

Indians were brought to the islands as indentured workers as were some Chinese. The latter in the main refused to stay as field workers and became shopkeepers. Since then they have met with variable levels of acceptance and hostility as economic conditions have varied within the Caribbean. For example, many lost their businesses during the late 1980s when a general worsening of economic conditions increased hostility towards minority groups.

Plantations still required labour and, from 1838 in Guyana, 1845 in Trinidad and 1854 in Jamaica, Indians still came as indentured workers. This continued until 1917 when the system was halted throughout the British Empire but between those years two and a half million Indians ventured abroad, half a million to the Caribbean (Vertovec 1994).

In turn, Jamaicans and Barbadians in large numbers were responsible for the labour used in building the Panama Canal. In the early 1950s and for the next two decades Caribbean citizens came to the UK. Sixty per cent were Jamaicans but other influences prevailed. In Bradford are to be found descendants of those from St. Lucia and St. Vincent whose French Catholic tradition also carries the flavour of the Spanish Main. Barbadians were recruited, with their government's support, to work in London Transport. The term 'diaspora' is commonly applied to Jewish wanderings and migration, and has been used in European literature to celebrate, dramatise and grieve for such pervasive, heroic and tragic dispersal of a culture. No less a term is worthy of the great Caribbean migration. This book looks at the children and, since the theme is dislocation, its traumas and triumphs, we focus on what for the child is the extreme situation, transition into the care of the state followed by the search for alternatives to the birth family. We set the scene by considering the concept of childhood within the United Kingdom where children have been valued yet exploited and abused, and, from the point of view of the law and health services, were until this century regarded as miniature adults.

During the 1960s the road back to the Caribbean became financially impassable for many immigrants. For example, in 1962 after a referendum, Jamaica turned down the chance to be a continuing part of the West Indies Federation which then soon ceased to exist. (Louise Bennett again: 'Dear departed federation, referendum murderation.') Although this fragmentation is still regretted the reality was, and is, for individual Caribbean islands, that political and economic isolation, rapid population increase, poor trading conditions for local resources such as aluminium ore, bananas and coffee, and loss of parity between Caribbean and US currencies led to steady falls in living standards.

Meanwhile, within the UK Caribbean immigrants, like those from the Indian and African continents, remained, in the main, fairly visible because of their skin colour. Negative discrimination occurred particularly in relation to housing and employment (accommodation to let signs often formerly stated 'No blacks or coloureds'). Recession, with the threat of continuing economic decline within the UK, diminished the financial value of the immigrant workforce and their children who, in the last decade of the century, include third and fourth generation descendants of the first arrivals.

This book focuses on particular ethical and legal developments of the late twentieth century and on a new vocabulary. Instead of the 'great big melting pot' of the ideal 1960s or 1970s society, with 'coffee-coloured people by the score', the aim defined by a popular song of the time, reformulated wisdom is that children from minority groups should be recognised as racially and culturally distinctive and should be brought up in, or at least with full knowledge of, the traditions, culture and religion appropriate to their origins. Concepts such as 'racial identity' and 'cultural heritage' are used as though they have clear-cut universally agreed meanings and as though these concepts are crucial to the well-being of children, a position which we question.

The word 'Negro', used matter-of-factly by the great Harlem-born American writer James Baldwin in 1966, is now regarded as pejorative. 'Patois' once also regarded as a pejorative term, now is used with pride. The word 'black' is used triumphantly yet simplistically when it is applied to people of Caribbean, African, Indian, Pakistani or mixed heritage. Other phrases used are 'black British', 'African American', and 'Afro-Caribbean'. Categorisations such as this confuse place of birth, place of residence, shades of skin colour, religion, culture and language, creating a 'great big melting pot' far more confusing and controversial than that of the original song.

In order to emphasise its theme of dislocation, this book starts with Chapter 1, a history of fostering and adoption services in the UK, with particular reference to the transition from adoption as a service providing babies to white Anglo Saxon parents to the development of facilities for children who formerly would have been considered too difficult to place with families. At one time early trauma or other disadvantages such as chronic or life-threatening illness or disability would have hindered the search for substitute parents. At first sight it would seem quite inappropriate to categorise children with different-coloured skins as having 'special needs' yet, when during the 1970s for the first time thought was given to finding permanent homes for children from ethnic minority groups, it was rare indeed to be able, even if this were thought desirable, to match parent and child. For a time a concept of 'colour-blindness' was fashionable and children from minority groups were difficult to place.

Chapter 2 places these issues in a historical context with regard to children's civil and legal rights.

In Chapter 3 we amplify our theme of 'colonisation in reverse' (Louise Bennett), the supply of human labour, the development of families within a matriarchal tradition rooted in the original diaspora from Africa, and the exploitation of the survivors of that rape of Africa, as colonial slaves.

This chapter sketches a picture illustrated by poems of the Caribbean from which its citizens derive their heritage. The islanders had history and colonial culture thrust upon them and for long thought that they could only copy it or have none of their own. But they can, to quote Derek Walcott, 'create their own histories'.

Chapter 4 records interviews by John J. Figueroa with achievers from Trinidad, Barbados, Jamaica and the other islands. He draws on these to delineate successful migrations and to contradict the West Indian stereotype, since it has been easier to recognise and to define short-term failure than to recognise longer term success. This chapter is about success and striving.

Chapter 5 considers family life, health and education in the United Kingdom and the West Indies, continuing and developing themes begun in the third chapter; the breakup of family networks, the effect of colonial traditions and slavery on the role of fathers, the social and economic difficulties of inner city life and the perception of black children in schools. Matriarchal patterns of family care did not survive well in impoverished inner cities, particularly when attempts were made to sustain them across three thousand miles of ocean, grandparents remaining in their born-islands. We discuss the prejudices and deficiencies which hindered the provision of effective school, health and social services and the effects upon children and second generation parents of dislocation and loss. We tell stories which illustrate these tragedies. Statistical evidence concerning this period is of limited quality and quantity, the discussion rather is of stereotyped impressions of Caribbean migrants and, for a crucial period during the 1970s, of refusal to identify national variety.

Chapter 6 draws on the report of a working party convened by the Child and Adolescent Psychiatry section of the Royal College of Psychiatrists, of which Jean Harris Hendriks was a member. Its brief was to consider the provision of child mental health services within a multi-ethnic society and principles of good practice in fostering and adoption, with particular reference to children from ethnic minority groups. Our first task indeed was to consider concepts such as 'ethnicity', 'culture', and 'identity'. We made a literature search on the concept of transracial family placement and tried to link this with the clinical and research basis for good practice in child psychiatry and social work. Now we ask whether 'race' is an inefficient concept even if 'racism' is not. We consider the voice of the child of mixed race and consider what may be learned from UK Caribbean children brought up in their birth families.

Chapter 7 attempts to define and delineate, via case histories and law reports, some of the bitter controversies that have arisen about the placement of children in other than their birth families. It draws on media discussions including those on inter-country and intercontinental adoption and tries to distinguish between what is known and what is a matter of prejudgment or over-rigid interpretation of limited knowledge. Some parts of this field are more clearly mapped than are others and the aim is that the range and depth of knowledge should be a matter for debate, not polemic.

Chapter 8 continues this theme by discussing the current legal system within the UK and how the civil rights of children may best be met within the framework of child law.

Chapter 9 reviews research on attachment, bereavement, dislocation and trauma in relation to children and their families.

Chapter 10 asks whether we have a baseline of knowledge about the needs and rights of all children for care, nurturance and education and about a hierarchy of knowledge on which we may draw when attempting to redeem the future for children when family life breaks down or they are otherwise dislocated. How may children be sustained in an environment in which they are safe and where attachments are available and reliable? How may these attachments be cherished and protected and, if a child may not live with its birth family, how may links be retained? Finally, how may we coordinate and develop, critically and without dogma, our understanding of the effects upon the well-being and mental health of children and their ethnic origin, religion, upbringing and cultural background?

It is important that we learn more of these issues as they affect young people within society and draw on and make use of that knowledge without allowing these factors to pre-empt or prevent the establishment of a sound and developing knowledge base concerning the health, well-being and education of all human children in any society. We ask how we may best avoid rigid ideological concepts yet cherish richness and diversity on behalf of all our citizens.

1 Bringing up other people's children

Surviving.
Just surviving.
Keeping it all at bay
and just having enough to pay
just enough to eat
just surviving on the little pay
and sending the kids to school.
   Where will the money come from.

Just surviving
      an yu cyaan see thru yu yeye
      fa yu just surviving
      on the little
      when you haven't any strength
         left in you body –

surviving.

('Surviving' by Maureen Ismay 1987)

Since the beginnings of human society children have been left parentless. Whether this happened through death, desertion, dislocation, kidnapping, slavery or natural disaster, the result for immature humans would be the same, death, unless some alternative care were offered, speedily and reliably. Many religions have enjoined charity to those less fortunate which can lead, as in Islamic law, to the rescue of abandoned children. The commonest event, were the child to survive, would be protection by the wider family.

Formal adoption used to be a service to the adopters rather than to the child. In Ancient Egypt, China, India and in Rome adoption was one of several ways in which an heir could be provided, ensuring the succession of wealthy families and that proper respect and religious rites towards ancestors would be sustained by legal heirs. Those who saw the film of Ben Hur will remember, besides the chariot race, that the former slave was adopted, in adult life, by a wealthy Roman, to be his heir. Benet (1976) has discussed sociopolitical aspects of adoption such as this.

In Europe, until the nineteenth century, the rescue of orphaned, abandoned, neglected or abused children remained within the province of charitable and religious foundations or of the state and what services existed were similar to those for adults. Services specific to childhood then began to develop as discussed in Chapter 2.

Here, we outline fostering and adoption in the UK as developed during the current century and in particular during the last four decades.

Going into care

A team of researchers at the Social Research Unit at Dartington, Devon has worked for several decades on this theme. Here 'care' equals care by the state acting in place of parents who were unavailable, dead, ill or incompetent. A hundred years ago, when earlier philanthropists attempted to help neglected, abandoned, deprived and abused children, it was thought that they had to be removed from neighbourhood and family. Children were taken into institutions, preferably far away from city streets, trained for service and apprenticeship and, until after the first half of this century, sent abroad as emigrants 'for their own good'. Little was known of the outcome, save that mortality rates were high, until the studies of institutional care described later in this chapter.

Who comes into care?

Recent research indicates that, though social deprivation and poverty in the UK are not of the order found by nineteenth century reformers, children received into the care of the state still come from very deprived families.

Bebbington and Miles (1989) studied 2,500 children in thirteen local authorities. They found only one quarter of the children had been living with both parents and three quarters of the families were on income support. One fifth owned the property in which they lived and more than half the children lived in deprived neighbourhoods. They compared two hypothetical children between the ages of five and nine years. The first child had a two-parent family, three or fewer siblings and lived in a house owned by his parents who did not depend on Social Security and with adequate accommodation. The odds on this child coming into care were, they calculated, one in 7,000. A child of the same age with one parent, of mixed ethnic origin, in crowded privately-run rented accommodation, on income support and with four or more siblings had a one in ten chance of coming into care.

The Dartington team (Millham *et al.* 1986) studied the likelihood that a child, once in care, would have to move on. They found that, of children looked after by a social services department for two years, forty per cent would experience a breakdown of placement and four-fifths of these took place as a crisis.

Rowe *et al.* (1989) compared the outcome of children in foster settings, residential placements and at home or with other relatives. They noted different risks under different circumstances. Foster placements were more prone to end abruptly, but when they could be maintained, were helpful and met their objectives better than residential placements which, though less likely suddenly to break down, failed to meet their objectives and were not seen, by social workers or children, as having been very helpful.

One fifth of children in care lose contact with their natural family (Millham *et al.* 1986). These workers studied 450 children who had entered care and found that those in residential and foster care who were in contact with their parents were 'less prone to crises and more competent socially and educationally'. Breakdown in contact happened when children were removed from turbulent households with many changes, changes which continued once the child had been separated. More than half the children in the study left care within three months but those who remained separated from their family were victims of neglect or abuse and troublesome adolescents. They found that contact declined partly because of geography and finance, partly because of family turbulence but, to a substantial extent, also because social workers visited less often and put less effort into maintaining contact between children and families, as time went by. The researchers thought that this was due to the constant pressure upon the workers to deal with fresh crises in other families. These children also did badly in terms of access to health and educational services (Bennathan 1992).

Despite this, and contrary to what is generally supposed to be the case, 90 per cent of the children studied eventually went home (Bullock *et al.* 1993). They found that these reunions took place despite the length of time the children had been away or the reasons for separation and that even young adults, some of whom had been abused or had themselves committed serious offences, would go back to their families even if this were only a brief stay. Indeed, such are the problems of young people who leave care, unsupported as young adults by reliable foster or adoptive families or by under-resourced social workers, that many are likely to drift back even to unsatisfactory home bases. The researchers emphasise that child protection services underestimate the pull of family and community even after long separation and in the face of abuse and neglect.

Three out of five children in the study went home within six months of being taken into care and of these about one fifth were only apart for about a week, presumably in response to some emergency. Eighty per cent of the children had been returned to their home within five years. The authors comment that this swift return of the majority of separated children is an unrecognised contribution by social workers to family welfare. The typical family is one temporarily unable to cope and other early returners are adolescents briefly separated from their home because they have been behaving badly.

They found that a child is more likely to return home if in foster care or a consistent residential placement, placed with the agreement of the family, has a mother who has provided emotional support, is placed with brothers and sisters and if parental illness was the main reason for the separation. Return home also depends on family-centered policies by the local authority and on whether the family is dependent on income support. The pull for return afforded by membership of an ethnic minority group may be still more potent.

The Dartington team point out that only five per cent or less of children separated from their families eventually are adopted and that nearly three years elapse between the time of separation and the adoption which is a period of great uncertainty for the child.

Permanency is more likely to be achieved with relatives. Thus, the range of fostering and adoption services for children exists within a matrix of families which weaves close links, persistent even when unreliable or inconsistent, with children received into care.

Fostering

Fostered children are brought up, for varying periods of time, away from their birth parents but the day to day caretakers do not have responsibility in the legal sense, this being retained by the birth parents, held by the state or shared between these two parties.

The earliest and longest-standing fostering arrangements have been between birth mothers and wet-nurses; babies being placed for breast-feeding with a foster mother. The baby might remain in the foster family for months or years, being visited at variable intervals by the birth parents or a wet-nurse might live within the household of the newborn, possibly to the detriment of her own children. Madame Bovary, in Flaubert's novel, visits her child at the home of the wet-nurse and these visits set the scene for encounters with an illicit lover. In *Dombey and Son* (1848), Dickens describes how the baby Paul, orphaned by the death of his mother in childbirth, is breast-fed by Polly Toodle who joins the Dombey household as a resident domestic. A sub-plot is the increasing deliquency of Polly's older son.

Beside informal emergency or long-lasting arrangements within families, fostering has become a service monitored and provided by the state. Foster carers in the UK are recruited, assessed, paid and supported by government departments, formerly children's departments, who trained and funded placement workers and, since 1971, by local authority departments of social services. Some foster parents recruited are relatives of particular children, offering their services, in a formal, financially supported way, to individual boys and girls whose story is known to them. This is a not uncommon arrangement where, for example, a single parent has died or is hospitalised and a sister or mother, with family commitments and limited resources, is able to take on additional child care with appropriate support. (The majority of child care is still undertaken by women.)

Other foster parents are recruited within a wider framework, being willing to take on a range of children for a variety of reasons, usually by negotiation with the Department of Social Services which has established a fostering scheme.

Short-term or emergency fostering

This may be offered to children where the parents need back-up because of illness, adversity and lack of support. Other avenues of help, such as the provision of residential family aides, would be explored in the hope that children could remain in their own home under such circumstances but failing this, short-term foster care, with the birth parent retaining full legal rights, would be seen by all concerned as an urgently necessary service to the children and their family.

Sometimes, there is no choice about the provision of emergency foster care; if children have been neglected, abused or abandoned, the primary concern is the provision of appropriate and immediate nourishment, warmth, care and protection.

Respite care

This is offered, within limited state resources, to families with special needs. Parents caring for a severely handicapped, chronically ill child may be helped by a foster family by whom care is offered so that birth parents may rest, recuperate and perhaps have more time for themselves and other children. This can provide opportunities for new friendships and experiences for child and family alike and, if birth parents at some time are ill or in difficulties, there is a known back-up service available for use in an emergency (York-Moore 1994).

Fostering with specific goals

Young babies may need temporary care while awaiting adoption placements. The foster families who take on the care of abused or neglected children may also help in the assessment of their needs by providing valuable information about sleep patterns, nutrition and development. Fostering is valuable to difficult teenagers and their families and some specialist fostering services provide short-term homes for young people who are not living harmoniously with their families and are not yet ready for independent living. In the right family children can learn more about themselves and how to manage their lives and relationships.

Long-term fostering

This is a term best applied to any situation in which a child lives away from his or her birth family for more than a few weeks. This rather rigid definition is of the greatest importance in the lives of small children since, for a two-year-old placed in foster care, a placement of six months equals one fifth of a life. A three-month-old baby, still in foster care on the first birthday, has then spent three-quarters of his life in 'temporary' care. Social workers talk of 'open-ended fostering' or 'drift' and attempt to guard against it. They are now supported in this by the wording of the 1989 Children Act (England and Wales) which enjoins upon children's courts and local authorities the duty to ensure that all hearings, and the making of plans concerning children, should take place within a relevant time framework, the welfare of the child being the paramount consideration. (See Mallucio *et al.* (1986) for discussion of the concept of permanency planning.)

Adoption

This began in the UK, as confirmed by the Adoption Act of 1926, as a service to childless families. Babies would be 'matched' with parents and, subsequent to the adoption, all legal ties with the birth parent or parents ceased forthwith. Adoption records were sealed and it was explicit that no contact could take place at any future time between the child and the birth family.

Then, in the last few decades as pointed out by Tizard (1977) and Clarke (1981), adoption has become an alternative form of child care, a complementary and more legally secure way in which children unable to live with their birth families can be brought up in alternative homes. What has happened therefore is that there are now new criteria for parents who apply for adoption. Forty years ago adoptive parents were expected to demonstrate that they were infertile and the health and racial origins and 'adoptability' (that is, the supposed acceptability as equivalent to a birth member of the family) of the child or the baby would be carefully considered. It was very rare for an older child to be placed and those with genetic disadvantage, chronic illness or handicap were not considered. Placement of children who were racially different from prospective adopters was almost unheard of. Thus, though very different from the adult adoptions of Ancient Rome, these legal arrangements were designed to meet the needs of adults who longed to be parents and who wanted children who looked as though they could have been born into the family. It was taken for granted that this would benefit the babies who would receive a better upbringing and education than could have been offered them under any other circumstances.

Children thought unsuitable for adoption were likely to be placed in institutional care. The change in adoption practice has taken place substantially because of increased understanding of the effects of institutions upon children and also because few babies are now available for adoption, as discussed later in this chapter. Longitudinal studies (Bohman and Sigvardsson 1980, Bohman 1981) also demonstrated the advantages of legal security in relation to improved outcome.

Institutional care

Traditionally, in the UK this has been available only to two groups of people, the children of the wealthy, placed by their parents in expensive boarding schools, often from as young as eight years old, and the very disadvantaged. The latter form of care, derived from nineteenth century workhouses and charitable institutions, as described by Dickens in *Oliver Twist, Nicholas Nickleby* and *Our Mutual Friend*, continued, though in less dire form and with more state regulation, into the twentieth century. During the 1930s and 1940s a number of classical studies described the effects upon children of living in large barrack-like 'children's homes'. The most striking feature was a gross abnormality in the development of relationships. Institutional children were shallow, over-friendly and unselective in their approach to unfamiliar adults, thus putting themselves at risk. They showed poor cognitive ability, did not do themselves justice educationally, had poor attention, many disturbances of habits and tended to be aggressive (Bender and Yarnell 1941, Bakwin 1949). As a result residential care at least in comparatively wealthy Western countries has in the last two decades become a rarity for under-fives but modern studies, for example on children in Romanian orphanages and in war zones, show comparable effects of current institutional care.

Adults who have been in such care can speak for themselves of their childhood. Triseliotis (1983a, 1983b, 1984, 1989) studied groups of young people fostered, adopted and brought up in institutions. They had in common a background of social deprivation, separations and moves between different types of placement and had parents with a history of social disadvantage, instability and in many cases alcohol abuse and criminality. On the whole, those in institutions or foster care were from the more disturbed backgrounds, having been 'held back' as unsuitable for adoption. However, they were articulate specifically about the effects upon them of institutional life. Nine out of ten said that they had missed the experience of growing up in a family and the majority described the impersonality of the institution, care-givers who came and went, rigid rules, lack of privacy and severe punishments. Growing up in an institution was seen as stigmatising and children in care because of family disadvantage found themselves branded as criminal or deliquent. This was not helped by a law (Children and Young Persons' Act 1969 England and Wales), benign in intent, which aimed to offer comparable services to children who had committed criminal offences and those who had not on the presumption that each group of children suffered from similar disadvantage. While this, broadly speaking, was true the net result was that the non-delinquent children became stigmatised as delinquent rather than that those who had committed crimes remained unlabelled.

Those young people brought up in institutions also complained that as parents they had great difficulty in coping with their young children. Quinton and Rutter (1988) also demonstrated that children who had received prolonged institutional care were more likely to have social difficulties and to make poorer parents in adult life.

Maria

Maria, aged 27 years, has given birth to two children, now aged eight and ten years, each of whom was adopted against her wishes. Maria, born in a rural Irish community, lost her mother to tuberculosis and was cared for in a convent-run orphanage from the age of three years. At 16 she moved from the orphanage into domestic service.

By the age of 17 years she had been introduced to heroin. Both of her babies were fathered by a violent man who has served a three-year prison sentence for stabbing Maria. After his discharge she rejoined her partner and is now again pregnant.

She has no stable relationships, has never worked since she was in service, has frequent temper tantrums and denies that her partner is any risk to herself or the unborn child. She says 'My husband and my baby are the only people in the world I can trust'.

Maria's older children were taken into care because of the risks to their health, safety and emotional well-being.

It is unlikely that her third child, when born, will be safe in her care. Maria's bereavement and institutional upbringing have left her unable to care for herself, let alone her children. Moreover, Maria is unlikely to be able to stay in contact with her baby because she insists that her partner, who recently has threatened the GP, Maria's social worker and the midwife, is no danger to anyone.

Thus, on top of the difficulties specific to growing up in an institution, however benevolent and well-meaning, are the further disadvantages that the young people, on leaving care, commonly have lost contact with their birth families and, as they reach legal maturity, also lose links with their institution, since charitable and state resources do not provide the kind of back-up that young people need and rely upon, even if at times they rebel against it, as they enter adult life (Millham *et al.* 1986). Since growing up in an institution also correlates with poor educational attainment (Jackson 1987), young people who leave care have quadruple disadvantages: poor self-esteem, lack of skill in making relationships, lack of roots and limited job opportunities. As with Maria, there are agonising decisions to be made about the safety of the next generation.

Modern trends in adoption and fostering

The range of services available to young people in trouble has been modified in relation to what is known about institutions but many problems continue. The main weakness in fostering services is that long-term care remains insecure, in partnership with the state via legal requirements and liaison with social workers and birth families and can be challenged, repeatedly, through court hearings. Not all young people wish to be adopted and not all families either could afford this or think it appropriate but Rowe *et al.* (1984) in a major study of long-term foster children found that even those who lived for between three and ten years in their alternative families were less secure than comparison groups of children in the general population and those who had been given the security of adoption. They concluded that foster care provides 'an insecure base for children to recover from earlier trauma or achieve their best development'. A more recent study (Rowe *et al.* 1989) showed little change.

Fratter *et al.* (1991) examined factors which increased the chances that a permanent placement away from home would break down. They found that the most vulnerable children were the older ones of mixed parentage who had been institutionalised and had a history of deprivation and abuse. Risk was increased if the children displayed behavioural or emotional difficulties, had multiple special needs and if they needed to keep up contact with brothers and sisters placed elsewhere yet not with their parents.

They considered that a child to whom four or more of these factors applied was many more times likely to experience a breakdown of their placement. In their view, continued contact with the natural family provided some protection in high risk situations.

Wolff (1987) outlines the knowledge base which will enable forward planning. The current need is for a framework which allows children to remain securely in alterative homes with or without adoption until adult life, in contact where appropriate with birth families and free from legal challenge or other continued uncertainty. (Thoburn 1988, 1989, discusses principles for good practice.)

Adoption: the changing pattern

In 1958 in the UK adoptions were at their peak and began to decline in numbers a decade later. Abortion became legal in 1968 and, over the next two decades, single motherhood became less stigmatised, financially more viable and, twenty years later the concept of illegitimacy disappeared from the legislature. Women had greater choice either to terminate a pregnancy or to retain their child. The greatest problem is economic disadvantage (Burghes 1994).

Over the same period, those adoptions which did occur changed in nature. More were of older children who were being adopted by natural parents and step-parents, a trend which reflects higher rates of divorce and remarriage since unmarried fathers and stepfathers may assume parental rights, alongside birth mothers, via the process of adoption.

The greatest change however, has been in the quality and kind of adoptions which do take place. These are now arranged as a service to children rather than to parents and the number of parents who would like to adopt exceeds the number of children available for adoption. Moreover, many of those children who are seeking, via local authorities or other adoption agencies, a permanent alternative home, are akin to those who twenty-five years ago would have grown up in institutions: children who have suffered dislocation, disadvantage, abuse, neglect or abandonment. Homes are now sought for children with special educational needs, health problems and disabilities where formerly this would have been thought inappropriate. A substantial literature attests to the success, overall, of these endeavours. For example, Kadushin (1970) discusses single parent adoptions and the adoption of older children. Macaskill (1985) outlines work on the adoption of children with severe learning disabilities and Wolkind (1979), Wolkind and Kozaruk (1983) on the adoption and foster care of children with illnesses and disabilities. Hersov (1990, 1994) provides an overview of historical issues, clinical and legal practice and research evidence. Wolkind and Rushton (1994) discuss, in similar terms, residential and foster families.

Inter-country adoption

The same trends which reduced the number of adoptions and changed its pattern and format in the UK had similar effects across the developed world.

Tizard (1991) reviews the pattern of inter-country adoption which started soon after the Second World War when children from Germany and other parts of war-torn Europe were sent, usually by religious organisations, for adoption in the USA and elsewhere in Europe. There was small-scale adoption between European countries for the next twenty-five years.

Orphans from the Korean and Vietnamese wars, plus children born of American soldiers overseas, were placed for adoption, mainly in the USA, until the early 1980s. This was a new form of charity, the desire to help abandoned and destitute children whose misfortune resulted from war but gradually also became a service for childless couples in the developed world who were unlikely to obtain babies for adoption within their native land.

This has given rise to a new and increasing controversy. On the one hand, parents who long for a child argue that they can offer much more than, for example, an orphanage in Romania or life on the streets in Brazil. On the other hand, international aid agencies and local governments stress that poverty, malnutrition and the effects of war should be dealt with in respect of whole populations rather than by a dramatic, somewhat romantic action in respect of individual children. To compound the problem, the scale of inter-country adoption is not known since many countries, including the UK, have not collected statistics.

Moreover, there is as yet no international legislation governing inter-country adoption and the countries from which the children come in the main are poor, but not the poorest in the world, yet have a high birth rate. It has been argued that under such circumstances this form of adoption is a new form of 'colonialism'. Developing countries may be offended by the implication that they cannot care for their own children. Moreover, there has been abuse in the form of child trafficking, with children bought and sold and problems within the framework of inter-country law of identifying when children are freely given up, when bought, and when taken without consent from their birth family. These problems in practice can be dealt with. The number of children involved is small and international legislation could, substantially, eliminate trafficking (Tizard 1991).

While it is true that in theory all children would be better cared for within their own country and many can, by persistent hard work, be found homes within their extended family, there are numbers of refugee orphans who do live for years in camps and without permanent carers. All the disadvantages which children suffer in the course of years of institutional care, as described above, apply irrespective of their birth country or language. Many large cities, for example in Latin America and India, have no support services whatever for street children and no extended families are available to care for them.

It would be doctrinaire therefore to prevent any form of inter-country adoption: the aim rather should be that the principles for practice to be described in our final chapter apply irrespective of a child's country of origin and prospective adopters should be assessed with equal rigour irrespective of the nationality of the child to whom they wish to offer a home. Laws, and child care services, must have an international component and all services for children be applied according to the Geneva and Hague Conventions. Tizard (1991) comments that, on the research available, the long-term outcome for transracially adopted children has been 'surprisingly good'. Commonly, the children are initially disturbed, with poor nutritional and health status, and many have experienced severe psychological trauma before arriving in their new home. They are likely to have experienced separations and, not uncommonly, two or more changes of language. They may be too young to understand and have lacked, in their own country, anyone available who could try to explain. Their physical environment and even the climate in which they live may be very different.

What is amazing, according to the range of research reviewed by Tizard, is that a majority of dislocated children do form attachments in their new homes and learn to communicate. The overall finding is that, just as in earlier studies of fostered, adopted and institutionalised children, legal security and persistence of care pay dividends. Such placements can work but of course should not ever be considered an alternative to wider socio-economic and political attempts to better the lot of all children in developing nations, the real cure for the evils which led to this debate about inter-country adoption.

Open adoption

Argent (1987, 1988) discusses early work on this theme. The term can describe a whole range of situations, from occasional supervised contact between a birth parent and a child, to frequent and informal visits between birth and adoptive families. The concept includes technically open access while emotionally there may or may not be close links between birth parent and child, or there can be an emotional openness, a willingness to discuss and understand roots and origins without face to face links. Van Keppel (1991) and Adcock *et al.* (1993) update the discussion.

Both publications describe the swing of the pendulum from the adoptions of the 1950s and 1960s, in which babies were handed over to adoptive parents without any identifying clothes or possessions from their birth homes, to an assumption that almost any child, in any permanent home, will benefit from regular face to face contact with members of the birth family. In time, the pendulum will settle somewhere between these two points with the overarching aim, as ever, that the rights and needs of individual children will be paramount when decisions are made concerning their well-being. There is need for further research, for example as a follow-up to that described by Fratter *et al.* (1991) to evaluate under what circumstances, for what children and with what frequency contact is of value, in what way such contact may hinder or enhance permanency planning and when such contact is likely in practice to prove hurtful, harmful or unrealistic.

Cullen (1994) discusses the judicial resolution of disputes about contact. As yet, there are no reliable statistics, but anecdotal evidence indicates that judges are prepared to make contact orders even in the face of the disagreement of the adoptive parents, a position which would have been unheard of until the Children Act came into force in 1991. It is of course very difficult in practice to enforce an order about which the recipients are unwilling but the principles in divorce court welfare work, where the starting point is that the child should have contact with both parents unless there are cogent reasons against it, has led to the robust making of orders in family proceedings even against the wishes of a parent with whom the child lives. A balancing act must be made where for example the settlement of the child in a step-family must be weighed against the loss to that child of contact for life with a birth parent, usually the father. The older the child the more weight is given to his or her wishes and it is recognised within the courts that older children cannot be coerced into contacts for which they do not wish (and that it may be difficult for them to express a wish for contact in the teeth of opposition from the parent with whom they live.)

The principle for practice is that, rather than conflictual and confrontational decision making, the aim should be to seek a framework whereby the door can be kept open, via indirect contact, intermediaries, via the possibility of future change as a child matures and new relationships become more secure and through judicial review. In adoption, the court will not be starting from the assumption that contact will take place, as will be the case in divorce or separation of birth parents, but with the hope that a combination of mediation, judicial review and more substantial post-adoption services will create an environment in which more flexible arrangements will be made, monitored and evaluated than has been possible to date.

This introductory chapter provides a brief overview of the range of services currently available for children and the world of family placement into which immigrant families have been drawn when in trouble and from which services may be requested in times of need. Since, almost inevitably, immigrant families have struggled with the disadvantages listed as particularly likely to create a situation where a child is taken into care, and since factors such as a child being of mixed race, with a history of deprivation and emotional difficulties, often may occur among recent arrivals in inner cities, there is a special need to study these factors, not because some families are of a different skin colour from the majority but because, for many immigrants, social difficulty and skin colour are linked, so that children are vulnerable.

Stories of care by the state

Ernest

Ernest, now eighty years old, became a Barnardo's boy when his mother died five years after his father was killed in the First World War. Ernest is the founder of a four-generation family and recently celebrated his golden wedding. He speaks with pride of his childhood and though he grew up without friendships from that time of his life and without direct links with the large country children's home in which he lived, he does have cherished photographs of the Barnardo boys' football team and a store of memories about the way of life. He reckons that he was always treated fairly and kindly and, since he has been a particularly loving husband, father and grandfather, it seems likely that his children's home which had a system of well established, reliable, long-serving house-parents gave him a sense of being valued. Also, he retains rich memories of his mother who cared for him when she was a widow and has a strong sense that he came into the world as a much wanted child.

Clara

Clara, aged fifty, being an in-patient with severe depression, speaks with rage of her children's home in which a house-father 'used to put his hands in our knickers and squeeze us'. She remembers being one of several girls who lived there between nine and sixteen years of age and that any of them was liable to be touched on the breasts and between the legs. This was never spoken about either between themselves or to other staff. Forty years later, she links her childhood with lack of joy in adult sexuality and increasing unhappiness.

Respite care

A general practitioner (York-Moore 1994) speaks movingly of the respite care which has helped himself and his wife to care for their son who has a rare genetic disability, to sustain themselves as a couple and to give time to their other children. He describes how a married couple have become their friends and that this relief family with grown up children offers visits for tea, weekends and up to a week at a time, which widen the horizons of their son and give peace of mind to his parents.

Angela

Since her mother was killed in a road accident Angela, aged eight, has been fostered with her mother's sister, husband and two small children. A fostering allowance is paid by her local authority to make this arrangement financially manageable. The plan was made with the agreement of Angela's father who works long and irregular hours but spends many visits with his sister-in-law and takes Angela on holiday. Angela's grandmother contacted Cruse, the association for the bereaved, and joined her granddaughter and the new family in the process of mourning. Angela is doing well and is likely to stay with her aunt until she is grown up.

Anna and Daniel

Many battles occur without reference to skin-colour or nationality. Anna was sixteen when she gave birth to Daniel. Anna's life was like that described by the Dartington Hall team. She was first taken into care when three years old when her own mother was hospitalised for depression. Her father, a heavy drinker, came and went from the family and several times assaulted Anna's mother who would press charges and then withdraw them. Anna was fostered five times between the ages of four and twelve years for periods varying from a few weeks to three months. By the age of fourteen she was truanting regularly from school and spent some time in a children's home. Daniel's father was a boy from the same children's home whose background was very like that of Anna.

Daniel was taken into care because he had a spiral fracture of the femur, an injury which, in a baby three months old, could not have occurred other than through mishandling. He was placed in a temporary foster home and the local authority planned that he should be adopted, mindful (as happened also with Maria) that they did not wish to see the baby enter the care pattern which had so damaged his mother and father. Anna, supported by her own mother, vehemently opposed this plan, saying that she wanted to give Daniel the care that she had never received herself. She also said that, if she could not look after Daniel, she wanted to play a part in his life and see him regularly throughout his childhood. A five-day court hearing was necessary to evaluate this conflict.

Chapter 9 outlines the knowledge base from which sounder practice must be developed, in order to resolve disputes such as that involving Anna and Daniel, to provide better quality respite care, with a pool of foster parents who can help children in need and their families, well-supported adoption services, including resources for contact post-adoption and group care for adolescents with family difficulties. A final chapter attempts to outline principles for practice concerning all children irrespective of their race, creed or colour.

2 What is childhood? A brief history of childhood and services provided for children

Children are easy to recognise (adolescents less so since the biological range may be from 11–19 years) yet definitions and concepts of childhood and adolescence vary greatly across time, place and social position. Children in general are seen as being innocent, dependent upon adults, needing to learn from them, to respect and imitate them and to fit in with their wishes, rules and instructions, adolescents as moving from within this framework towards adult life, albeit with difficulty.

Evidence concerning the history of childhood, even within comparatively literate and developed societies, is patchy and incomplete, depending as it does on the historical interpretation of literature, art and contemporary records. By definition, little can be learned about the family life of those who are inarticulate and illiterate. Inevitably, historical writing is selective. Two very different accounts are those of de Mause (1976) and Aries (1962), respectively American and French social historians.

De Mause has written: 'The history of childhood is a nightmare from which we have only recently begun to awaken. The further back in history one goes, the lower the level of child care and the more likely children are to be killed, abandoned, beaten, terrorised and sexually abused'. He outlines stages from a grim past to a benevolent present in which we have become able to understand and accept children as separate beings from adults, with special needs, rights and values. He regards the 'helping' of children as the result of an evolutionary process. It has been argued that it was emotionally unsafe, until post-medieval times, for parents to love their children because the emotional investment, in a time of high infant mortality, carried with it such intolerable risk.

Other writers, drawing heavily on literature and art, recognise that this is a retrospective falsification and that grief at the loss of much-loved children has been an ever-recurrent theme. Children were seen as an important source of love and satisfaction as they were growing up and of help and comfort in old age. Only in the most extreme of circumstances of social disadvantage were these feelings lost or distorted.

In the tenth century the Japanese woman poet Shikibu wrote, on the death of her daughter:

> From darkness into the path of darkness.

Shakespeare wrote:

> Grief fills the room up of my absent child,
> Lies in his bed, walks up and down with me;
> Puts on his pretty looks, repeats his words,
> Remembers me of all his gracious parts,
> Stuffs out his vacant garments with his form.

> (*King John*, Act III Scene 4)

Robert Burns, the eighteenth century poet, who knew at first hand about rural labour and hardship, wrote:

> Fate gave the word, the arrow sped,
> And pierced my darling's heart
> And with him all the joys are fled
> Life can to me impart.

> (A Mother's Lament for the Death of her Son)

Aries has been quoted as saying that the concept of childhood is comparatively a recent one. This is so, in that his accounts of medieval society are of children who mingled with adults as soon as physically they were able to do this and who spent their time in a wider community both at work and at play, learning by instruction and imitation and gradually becoming responsible and active contributors to community life. De Mause in contrast sees children as victims, commonly cruelly treated, undervalued and as being offered but limited amounts of love and affection lest the agony of loss be too great for endurance. Aries (1962) writes, more moderately: 'The idea of childhood is not to be confused with affection for children: it corresponds to an awareness of the particular nature of childhood ...'. He considers that parents loved their offspring without sustaining a formal concept of childhood.

As ever, reality is somewhere between extremes. Children always have been subject to abuse, neglect and exploitation and always have been valued as important members of and potential contributors to the society in which they live as well as being valued for themselves. Sources inevitably are limited; *The Penguin Book of Women Poets* (Cosman *et al.* 1978), from which the Japanese quotation is taken, consists, inevitably, at least until the eighteenth century, of the fortunately preserved writings of articulate, privileged, upper class women. It took a Robert Burns to speak for the bereaved cotter's wife.

Confusion has arisen because the concept of childhood as a social construct differs from the process of loving and caring for children. It is indeed an important by-product of that process since legal, social, educational and health services have evolved in a more equitable and effective way as they became targeted towards an identified social group with rights and needs.

Children have been loved, valued, taught, protected and also exploited, neglected, abused, undervalued or seen as expendable in different societies for different reasons and at different times since records have been kept. De Mause sees the concept of childhood as having benefited the young whose rights and needs are identified and whose caretaking has been improved as society has evolved and become more complex. Aries, on the other hand, sees children as having done better when they were active, valued members of a society and as at risk of being repressed, undervalued and marginalised once the concept of 'childhood' became crystalline and constricting.

It is possible to imagine some idyllic Caribbean life in which children, like those in seventeenth century England, were accepted in home, yard, farm and workplace, gradually acquiring skills along with their elders although they would also be taking the risks of illness, injury or accident common to all members of their community. It is likely that this would be as simplistic as the current ill-informed political notion of a 'Victorian England' to whose values we must return. It was indeed the lot of bereaved, abandoned, neglected and impoverished children in the nineteenth century in England which led to the development of charitable foundations and the establishment of law which combined to identify childhood as a period in life requiring services both specialised and specific and to set the scene for modern health, education and social services which, in principle at least, are now available to all children of any nationality within our society.

Children and the law

Here we begin to understand the confusion which still exists around the concept of childhood. For example, within the three jurisdictions of the United Kingdom plus the Republic of Ireland, there is variation regarding the age at which a child may be considered 'criminally responsible', able to answer within a court of law to charges of wrongdoing. In Eire the age of criminal responsibility is seven years though in reality the younger age group is allowed, via a formality, the presumption of incapacity and is offered free legal aid. In Northern Ireland, England and Wales the age of criminal responsibility is ten years whereas in Scotland it is eight years yet, there, a system of family courts deals informally with most juvenile crime so that the legal concept of criminal responsibility in practice is largely irrelevant.

Children can be treated as legal adults, from the point of view of sentencing, once they reach the age of seventeen years in Ireland, England and Wales, and in Scotland at the age of sixteen years (Stewart and Tutt 1987).

In civil law the upper age of childhood is eighteen years, yet in England and Wales, with parental consent, young people can marry once they are sixteen. The law on driving, the consumption of alcohol, consent to medical intervention or to sexual acts varies widely between jurisdictions.

Historically, and in developing or poorer countries, childhood is a briefer construct and adolescence under-recognised. The poorer the country the more readily children are required to assume adult responsibilities at an earlier age. In the 'developed' world young people are kept in education longer, a response to the reduced requirement for manual labour, increased unemployment and the need for a better-trained work-force capable of coping with sophisticated technology.

Children and education

In 1863 Charles Kingsley, a clergyman born in 1819, wrote about Tom, a small boy exploited as a chimney sweep, and abused and beaten by his master and near-owner Mr Grimes. Tom had already twice been sent to prison by the local squire, there being no duty to think about the age of criminal responsibility, children being treated as adults if they were lawbreakers. Kingsley wrote about the education of children in the form of a fairy story, which like all the best fairy stories really is meant for adults. Tom acquires a complex, lengthy education in morality, responsibility, science and language, the root of which is the importance of human relationships. Kingsley probably had read in Dickens' *Hard Times*, published in 1854, an attack on the false educational premises which regarded the children of the poor as objects to be controlled, fed with facts and fitted for manual labour. As Ackroyd writes in his biography of Dickens (1990): 'The horrors of a childhood unalleviated by fancy could be aligned to the horrors experienced by the urban poor and by the working people of the great industrial cities'.

In 1870 education became compulsory with a system of national schools and inspectors. Flora Thompson (1945) described the standardised examinations in scripture, reading, writing and arithmetic undergone in ritualistic ordeal by children who would leave school and enter the adult world at twelve years of age.

Universal teaching, with access to higher education and university according to merit became a near-realised ideal of the mid-twentieth century, now again at risk via partial privatisation, neo-Victorian values idealised by the historically illiterate and financial constraints. Paradoxically, there is now an argument that the school-leaving age of sixteen years is too high; what was seen in the 1960s as increased freedom and flexibility for children offering educational opportunity far beyond that available in any previous generation, may now be over-restrictive, restraining people from entering adult life and responsibilities yet becoming too inflexible for those for whom education throughout their lives should be a goal and privilege.

The majority of those entering the UK from the Caribbean joined our educational system during this paradoxical period of increased rigidity, in that to be out of school under the official school-leaving age became a status offence (that is, one which can only be committed by people who fall within pertinent categories, in this case a specific age range). They did this while themselves leaving, having left, or having been brought up by parents who took part in, an educational system which was at the same time less rigid and more restricting. Today's children are protected and educated, prolonged adolescence is a privilege, a burden, an inappropriate empowerment and a restriction. Perhaps, from the point of view of education, matters have not changed since Shakespeare wrote in *The Winter's Tale*: 'I would there were no age between sixteen and three-and-twenty, or that youth would sleep out the rest; for there is nothing in the between but getting wenches with child, wronging the ancientry, stealing, fighting'.

Stewart and Tutt (1987) write: 'The welfare system of child protection and deliquency control has been more concerned with who children are rather than what children do'. They point out that the construct of childhood is 'capable of change and redefinition as social attitudes shift'. Provision of education, child protection and social services for children has varied over time as does family life and structure. This process, which has perhaps accelerated during the last two centuries, continues. Identifiable trends are an increasing dependence of the family on the state, the availability of specialised agencies to fulfil some of what formerly were the functions of a family, particularly as it became recognised that the family could not sustain all that was needed or could be an agency of abuse and neglect. Children's rights increasingly have been emphasised, a process which in the UK has culminated in an extensive revision of the law, parental authority has declined (the Children Act 1989 (England and Wales) speaks of responsibilities, not rights). The role of women has changed both in and outside the home, a process, which continues and, in theory at least, both parents are required to take a sustained and responsible role in the rearing of children.

Murch and Hooper (1992) outline some of these changes in demographic form. In England and Wales the number of divorces increased sixfold between 1960 and 1980, rising to 160,000 by 1985 and then levelling at around 150,000 per annum. It is now estimated that if these trends continue 37 per cent of all marriages will end in divorce. The writers comment that these figures are not a reflection of marriage breakdown since, before 1960, the majority of failed marriages ended either informally or with the application to magistrates courts for separation orders. Nevertheless, it is of great significance that two-thirds of couples who divorce have dependent children and it is projected that one in five of all children will have experienced parental divorce by the time they are sixteen years of age; these figures may reduce only in relation to a complementary and increasing trend for cohabitation, with partnerships informally beginning and ending unrecognised by legal sanctions.

A family group may now consist of 'his, her, our and their' children, with non-resident parents and complicated extended families.

It is ironic that the variety and flexibility of family settings within the UK often now mirror the substantially matriarchal child-rearing patterns brought to us from the Caribbean which, thirty years ago, stood out as idiosyncratic within the host society.

The changing pattern of educational provision must be seen in the context of changing family patterns. Today's teenagers, whatever their racial origin, are more likely than ever before to live in complex reconstituted families and to take part in an educational system, compulsory until they are sixteen years of age, which is insufficient to prepare them for a lifetime of changing work conditions and limited employment prospects.

Children and mental health

This is an uncertain, unreliable world, yet this has been the case for children and their parents in all societies and over time. It is surprising therefore that the scientific study of childhood is a recent event and that paediatrics did not emerge as an organised medical speciality until the mid-nineteenth century. Charles Dickens, who campaigned for health services for children, described the opening of the Great Ormond Street Children's Hospital in 1852, when he wrote his last complete novel, *Our Mutual Friend* (1865). These early hospitals did not provide for children in mental or emotional distress and early literature on childhood insanity is sparse; the limited references which are available occur within the writings of physicians specialising in the insanity of adult life (Parry-Jones 1989, 1994). Children were admitted to prisons, like Tom in *The Water Babies* or to workhouses like Oliver Twist (Dickens 1837), and only rarely, and in extreme cases to lunatic asylums such as the Hospital of St Mary of Bethlehem, London (Bedlam), perhaps at the rate of two or three children per year. During 1897 Oscar Wilde, in Reading gaol, saw child rabbit poachers in prison uniforms which enveloped them. A warder was dismissed for giving the smallest child a biscuit when he cried for hunger (Hyde 1976).

The twentieth century saw a coming together of health, education and social services in relation to child health. The pressures came, not so much from hospital-based paediatrics as from school health services, where standards of nutrition and cleanliness were in question, from educationalists who began the task of evaluating children's 'innate capacity' and, most influentially, from the juvenile justice system. It was no longer thought appropriate that children, whatever the debate about their capacity to understand right and wrong and to accept responsibility for their actions, should be punished as though they were already full adults. These combined influences led in the 1920s to the establishment of what was then called the Child Guidance Movement (it is no coincidence that an early American clinic was entitled the Judge Baker Clinic, endorsed by the legal system above all others; many beside Oscar Wilde had seen children in prison). In these clinics there was interdisciplinary partnership between psychiatrists developing their speciality of working with children, psychologists and social workers. An attempt was made to put together these fields of knowledge and to distinguish between the medical study of children who in some way deviated from the norm, the range of normal behaviour and capacities, the field of the psychologist and teacher, and the context in which the child lived and developed, the province of the social worker. In those early days the context was seen as the mother first, the family second and society third, priorities which have changed and become more subtle with the passage of time. The task was seen as helping a growing child to adjust to his immediate environment, hence the name of the service (Harris Hendriks and Black (1990) edit an overview of child and adolescent mental health services in the UK).

These concepts, though simplistic and in need of modification and development, are insufficient and indeed harmful if allowed to hinder the study of child mental health and illness from a scientific viewpoint which takes account of genetics, biological investigation, systematic classification and epidemiological study. According to Parry-Jones (1994) modern students of child psychiatry have under-estimated earlier medical understanding of child development and the significance of life experiences and influences such as changing parent–child relationships. He stresses the need to place historical facts within the ethos and value systems of their contemporary culture. He emphasises the role of doctors as well-trained medical specialists in the development of a range of services for children which draws on knowledge of psychology, social work, criminology, hospital and community-based services for children and services for those with learning disabilities and handicaps. One may add to this, the need to understand and provide such services across boundaries of race and language.

Children as witnesses
(see Spencer and Flin 1993)

It has been difficult for children to contribute to the legal process. In courts of law, until the Criminal Justice Act 1991 (England and Wales), a child who was to be a witness was examined by a judge as to 'competency'. The judge had to form an opinion as to whether the child did or did not understand the difference between truth and falsehood and the importance of telling the truth. The new law, which is responding to much better knowledge about how children observe and remember (they are working from a smaller base of experience and knowledge but are developing the same range of skills as the adult population) set up a system whereby any child who could communicate in an intelligible way was considered competent to give evidence in a criminal court. All children under fourteen are now asked to give their evidence unsworn.

This is of the greatest importance concerning the civil rights of children who should be taken seriously and listened to if they have witnessed crimes or been victims of crime either inside or outside their homes. Their evidence, of course, is also important if they are accused of criminal activities. For example, the many children who have witnessed violence, such as those described by Straus *et al.* (1990), Harris Hendriks *et al.* (1993) and Mama (1994), are capable, if asked, of describing their experiences with far greater accuracy and detail than hitherto has been supposed possible. Young children can express what they have experienced via drawing, acting and play as well as in words. Moreover, even very young children, as they mature, may be able to recollect and describe in words experiences which happened when their verbal abilities were very limited.

All of this is of the greatest importance concerning the civil rights of children in the wider field of legal decision making, for example when they are in need of protection after abuse, and may claim compensation, or they may need alternative families, when they may be placed long-term in foster or adoptive homes, or when there are decisions as to where they will live and which relatives they will see on a regular basis after divorce.

Children must give their own permission for medical or psychiatric evaluations 'according to their age and understanding', thus a court or a parent cannot order a child to have medical treatment or undergo an examination for a court against the child's wishes unless there is a life-threatening situation or the child is incompetent, either through being very young or through being too ill, to understand the issues involved. The focus today therefore is on an obligation to communicate with children, help them to understand the procedures in which they are involved and to hear from them directly about what their experiences have been, rather than for adults to decide on the children's behalf what they need, what they have experienced and what will be best for them in the future. These rights and duties of children of course do not override or blot out the duties of parents, guardians, physicians and lawmakers; the aim rather is that children should be included in the process rather than passively receive it.

When an adult may speak for a child, for example as a guardian ad litem or advocate in court proceedings, the obligation on the advocate is to communicate as effectively as possible with the child and with all of those who care for him. If a doctor decides to override a decision made by a child about whether to undergo a medical procedure or examination, the doctor must exercise reasonable care, consult the adults involved, think of taking the views of colleagues if there is likely to be controversy and carefully record what the decision is and why it has been made.

Thus, those who want to work with children in law, education or health services now have an obligation to consider the child's age and understanding (this is dealt with in more detail in Chapter 9), to listen to what the child has to say, and to take it most seriously, particularly when the child may have witnessed, or been accused of taking part in, criminal activity, and to obtain the child's consent for procedures which involve him. Children may and ought to be taken seriously as witnesses in a court of law. The criteria for their involvement should be that the children have knowledge or information which may be useful to a court and that they are able to communicate. Today courts are attempting to make this easier for children by using screens or video links and by allowing a child to have a trusted adult within reach when evidence is given. There is a long way to go, and currently there is controversy indeed as to whether the pendulum has swung too far 'towards the rights of children' and away from the rights of parents, guardians and teachers, but the debate is a healthy and important one which will continue. Overall, today children are less likely to be treated as members of a minority group and more likely to be regarded as citizens of the state in their own right.

Services for children have grown in a piecemeal way, over time, often in response to charitable impulse and sometimes have been influenced by fashion, dogma or inadequate, ill-understood information and some historical misconception, all of which also may affect current and future policy making. The overarching need, in the fields of criminology, education and child health and social services, is for good quality practice, informed by well-documented and evaluated research and underpinned by sound, regularly revised laws concerning the rights of children and adolescents; a theme to which we will return.

3   Colonisation in reverse: a Caribbean heritage

Although we are all brothers
Especially
In the bondage of our skin,
A forced fellowship smothers
Fraternity,
For we are by no means all akin.

Don't abrade what's already rough;
Be kind
To our children, do, man!
It's quite difficult enough
They'll find
Just to cope with being human.

(A.L. Hendriks, Paper to a Black Power Conference,
unpublished)

Not all minority cultures are linked with skin colour, in the UK
Cockneys, Yorkshiremen and Scots are all white-skinned with dif-
fering cultures, traditions and dialects. They are not the same as
Essex man. When considering people of Caribbean heritage (CH)
there are some basic matters which have to be stated rather baldly.
The first is the common misconception that Jamaica makes up the

whole of the Anglophone or post-British West Indies, and a second is that the islands of the Caribbean are part of Africa (see Louise Bennett's 'Back to Africa,' below), thirdly, cultures change even if slowly and the Jamaica of today, like other Caribbean islands, is very different from that from which, in the late 1940s and early 1950s, people flocked to England in search of a British life.

Many of the Caribbean heritage families now living in the UK came here before the black power movement arrived from the USA to the West Indies. Early immigrants had been brought up to think of themselves as British, and this despite the influence of people such as Marcus Garvey, a Jamaican journalist and politician, who, in 1919, founded the Universal Negro Improvement Association of the World aimed at 'asserting the dignity of the Negro' in both the New World and Africa. (Note that unselfconscious use of the word Negro.) From Trinidad, George Padmore, C.L.R. James and Sylvester Williams, in the early part of the century, played a leading part in the pan-African movement, aimed at what later would be called raising the consciousness of the black Caribbean population and at reinforcing and emphasising links with Africa (James 1968). At the same time in the French-speaking Caribbean man Aimé Césaire from Martinique created the concept of 'negritude' that was to have a profound effect on black consciousness movements world-wide.

This USA/Caribbean/African cultural and political movement derived not only directly from parts of Africa, but also from the history of slavery. Yet much of the Caribbean has always been multi-cultural, since its various exploitation by European powers and, one hundred and thirty years after the slave trade was banned, the rush of Caribbean people to Britain was linked rather with powerful and pervasive economic influences, enhanced, at least in the 'British' West Indian islands, by an educational tradition substantially imported from the UK which concentrated far more on Anglo-European history, geography and trading patterns than on African or Caribbean history (Manley 1974).

Not long after slavery was abolished (1838) in the British West Indies, to be followed by the importation of indentured labourers from India and China, English people, Irish labourers, Scottish housekeepers and French and English owners of estates and slaves settled, willingly or unwillingly, in the West Indies. Until thirty years ago various British soldiers and sailors manned garrisons. Thus, little more than a hundred years separated the abolition of slavery and the beginning of the big rush to the UK. People who came from the Indian subcontinent to the Caribbean were both Hindu and Muslim and a number of them converted to Christianity, especially to Presbyterianism. As Dr Eric Williams (1955), historian and former Prime Minister of Trinidad, put it, 'unfree labour in the Caribbean was black, white and brown; Protestant, Catholic and pagan'. But of course in Britain all this mixture of cultures and religions, shaken up together in small islands, is designated Afro-Caribbean. It is suggested that if you are from the Caribbean you must be black and if you are black you must be African. It is the same sort of language magic that until lately kept Australia so far from the Pacific in which it breathes; most of the inhabitants (that counted) were white, therefore they were European.

A similar sort of language magic now has it, if the state has any say in the matter, black or brown children must be placed with at least one black or brown parent. Other options may not be sought, or even considered.

One aspect of culture which was strong among those who came nearly fifty years ago from the Caribbean was the extended family. There was a whole network of support for the care of children; the kingpin of this network was usually Grannie. If Mother could not cope because, for instance, she had gone into domestic service, or simply gone away, her mother or sisters, sometimes living in the country, would take over the upbringing of the child despite pressures from poverty or heavy family commitments, so that George Lamming's (1953) 'it was my mother who fathered me' could often be extended to 'it was my grandmother who mothered me'. Auntie also played an important part. A well known personality who was brought up by his aunt, at least to some extent, was the great West Indian cricketer George Headley. He was born in Panama of a Barbadian father and a Jamaican mother. The mother moved with George to Cuba in search of a better life. But when George was about eleven or twelve years old she wanted him to have British education, and not to grow up speaking Spanish. She therefore sent him to his aunt in Jamaica. His father does not feature in any of the stories told about him. But one should note that in the more recent culture of places like Jamaica the father is playing a more important role in the upbringing of children.

The Headley case reminds us that migration for West Indian people did not start with the influx into England which, if you listened to the press, to some prelates and politicians, was about to swamp the (mythical) good, old and monolithic English culture. To begin with, as is beautifully put by Collymore's 'Triptych' (see below), the vast majority of West Indian people were dragged to the islands, once the original population had been reduced to a minimum, by slavery or indenture or poverty or by escape from failed revolutions. It is in their culture to travel to look for a better life.

What made the journey to England more difficult than to many other places was first of all the xenophobia endemic in English culture – note that much of the country still has no doubt that the whole of the continent of Europe is inferior. One aspect of this xenophobia was racism. But a bigger problem probably was that, England being highly industrialised, individualistic and competitive, there were few networks of any kind to help if things went wrong. Even fifty years after the first heavy influx of 'coloureds' from the Caribbean, native English women are still fighting for suitable nursery schools and creches which they need as the community becomes more 'competitive', and more women find that they must go out to work. In this matter the Government seems to say that it cannot afford nursery education, but one could be forgiven for supposing that it really thinks that nursery education should be part of the employment 'package' which firms offer in their competition for staff. Economic disadvantage for the natives bears yet harder on newcomers. Even when things were 'improved', they were upsettingly different.

One of the changes which people who grow up in the tropics have to face on coming to developed northern countries is that in the tropics there is little distinction between the inside and the outside of a home. The street or the yard or the pavement is very close to being part and parcel of the house. Roaming the street or running down the road are part of growing up in the Caribbean, they may be considered vagabondish and antisocial in a place like England, especially in big industrial cities. Clearly for adolescents this presents many problems, not least of all with 'new' hardly known fathers and the police, problems described in Chapter 5.

Of course now many young people who are called black or West Indian will have been born in the UK, but their culture might not be fully UK because of the influence of their parents and of living in ghettos inhabited almost entirely by West Indian Heritage people. Also the way 'native' English people look at them, and what they expect from them, affects the image which they have of themselves, as described by the teenagers interviewed by Tizard and Phoenix (1993) and discussed in Chapter 6.

Some West Indian parents, having found the UK disappointing and difficult, give their children a rather rosy spectacled view of 'back home'. Yet in many ways home has changed remarkably, not only politically but also socially and economically: Trinidad and Tobago is now a Republic, and in Jamaica there has been serious talk of seeking such a form of government. In both places, and especially in Jamaica, there has been an increase in public violence, and in both, together with Barbados, heavy drugs and trafficking in them are changing what used to be difficult and poor environments into gun-happy and dangerous ones.

But, perhaps because migration from the Caribbean to England has almost ended, the present state of Caribbean culture is not of great significance to Caribbean heritage people now living in the UK (except when Jamaican 'yardies', involved in drug trafficking and violence, are publicised in the UK media) and, much more significantly for individual families, where their heritage contains elements which have persisted for many years such as the sustaining of extended family links and the delight in young children. Sadly, along with that delight goes as often severe thrashing of older children which when it manifests itself in the UK quite rightly causes amazement and disapproval. Beating children is wrong and not acceptable within any cultural framework.

For many UK Caribbean families their extended family remains in the Caribbean; community networks for children in the UK have hardly yet been built up, nor sustained.

One must stress again the variants in the culture of the Caribbean. True there are common factors connected with sugar production, dependence on one or two primary products, and colonialism in general. But there are differences in language, religion and general culture which have to be respected: they tend to be forgotten in the UK where there is an impression that all Caribbean people come from Jamaica! This impression continues despite fairly popular knowledge of a 1990s West Indies cricket team which contained Lara from Trinidad, Richardson and Ambrose from Antigua, Walsh from Jamaica, Haynes from Barbados, and Chandipaul from Guyana. This last name is worth noting for his ancestors, and therefore one strand of his culture, came from the subcontinent of India, and not from Africa or Europe. Adams is now playing county cricket in England: his mother is from Canada, while his father is a medical doctor in Jamaica.

Among West Indian writers, three of the most famous are Walcott, Naipaul and Brathwaite: these are respectively from St Lucia, Trinidad and Barbados. Walcott's journey to the Nobel Prize for Literature (1992) took him from his French Creole roots in St Lucia, via Trinidad, to the world stage; his epic poem *Omeros* (1990) symbolises and transcends all such journeys. Similarly, Naipaul left the black/Creole/East Indian world of Trinidad to study life in India itself and wrote his greatest novels as an expatriate in the UK. *The Middle Passage* (1962), an early contribution to a series of distinguished novels, struggles with bitterness, regret and irony which characterise the chameleon-like adaptation of a Hindu West Indian to English life. Edward Brathwaite was educated in Barbados and at Cambridge University but his first job as an educator in Ghana, West Africa was critical to his future writing which, as symbolised by his replacing the name Edward with the name Kamau, has led him to focus on connections between language, culture and customs in West Africa and those in the Caribbean. Perhaps the problem is really a geographical one. Few people in the UK woud realise that Jamaica is in a different time zone from Barbados and 1,200 miles from Trinidad and Tobago. Homeric journeys may take place within the Caribbean, across the Atlantic to the UK and in search of origins in India and in Africa.

The fact that all Caribbean people, including even the Jews and Chinese (see Chapter 4), are likely to look 'black' to racialist Britain is no reason to believe that in culture, religion and upbringing they are likely to be identical and easily substitutable in the adoption and fostering business, or as role models to UK West Indians. Nor will they be unaccustomed to knowing Caribbean families in which the mother might be white while the father is black, and the children all shades according to the way in which genes distribute 'colour'.

In looking at the present day situation of Caribbean heritage people in the UK one has to remember that most children now in school will have been born here: their *grandparents* migrated to the UK. These young people will not have suffered from the migratory experience – not in the way in which some years ago a child of seven might have, on being sent to England to his 'parents' only to find that he does not recognise his mother's partner as the father he dimly remembers or as an instant stepfather.

Present day children may have suffered from racism or simple xenophobia, as well as from the general feeling that after school there will be no jobs. And their parents and grandparents may give them a false view of how paradisiacal life is in the West Indies compared to the UK. But the expectation that they must be poor performers will not be as strong as it was for the former migrants. For, as we shall see in the next chapter, not a few West Indian heritage people have now been achievers in the UK. But the need and aim must be to eschew all prejudged images, even though we know that there are bound to be likenesses among people sharing cultures and general experiences, especially work experiences. The lack of family networks, of grandparents and aunts who are not working, and are willing to take over children while their parents, or *parent*, struggle to make a living, must make a difference. But different families will try to cope with this and other difficulties in various ways – one or two have even taken the fairly drastic step of sending children back to their Caribbean families, and these families will certainly differ depending on what territory is in question, and what standard of living is enjoyed.

West Indian poets have expressed the mixture of cultures and peoples who make up the Caribbean. Beyond a doubt a small selection of their work might cause even 'Black Caucuses' to recall what the Caribbean heritage really is.

Holy

Holy be the white head of a Negro,
Sacred be the black flax of a black child.
Holy be
The golden down
That will stream in the waves of the winds
And will thin like dispersing cloud,
Holy be
Heads of Chinese hair
Sea calm sea impersonal
Deep flowering of the mellow and traditional.
Heads of peoples fair
Bright shimmering from the riches of their species;
Heads of Indians
With feeling of distance and space and dusk:
Heads of wheaten gold,
Heads of peoples dark
So strong so original:
All of the earth and the sun!

(George Campbell, Jamaica)

Back to Africa

Back to Africa Miss Matty?
Yuh no know wa yuh dah sey?
Yuh haffe come fron some weh fus,
Before yuh go back deh?

Me know sey dat yuh great great great
Gramma was African,
But Matty, doan yuh great great great
Grampa was Englishman?

Den yuh great granmada fada
By yuh fada side was Jew?
An yuh grampa by yuh mada side
Was Frenchie parley-vous!

But de balance a yuh family
Yuh ole generation
Oonoo all bawn dung a Bun grung
Oonoo all is Jamaican!

Den is weh yuh gwine Miss Matty?
Oh, you view de countenance,

An betweens yuh an de Africans
Is great resemblance!

Ascorden to dat, all de, blue-eye
Wite American,
Wa great granpa was Englishman
Mus go back a Englan!
Wat a debil of a bump-an-bore,
Rig-jug an palam-pam!
Ef de ole worl' start fe go back
Weh dem great granpa come from!

Ef a hard time yuh dah run from,
Teck yuh chance, but Matty, do
Sure a weh yuh come from so yuh got
Someweh fe come-back to!

Go a foreign, seek yuh fortune,
But no tell nobody sey
Yuh dah go fe seek yuh homelan
For a right deh so yuh deh!

(Louise Bennett, Jamaica)

In our land

In our land,
Poppies do not spring
From atoms of young blood,
So gaudily where men have died:
In our land,
Stiletto cane blades
Sink into our hearts,
And drink our blood.

In our land,
Sin is not deep,
And bends before the truth,
Asking repentantly for pardon:
In our land,
The ugly stain
That blotted Eden garden
Is skin deep only.

In our land,
Storms do not strike
For territory's fences,
Elbow room, nor breathing spaces:

In our land,
The hurricane
Of clashes break our ranks
For tint of eye.

In our land,
We do not breed
That taloned king, the eagle,
Nor make emblazonry of lions:
In our land,
The black birds
And the chickens* of our mountains
Speak our dreams.

(Harold M. Telemaque, Trinidad)
*chickens: chicken hawks

Triptych

I see these ancestors of ours:
The merchants, the adventurers, the youngest sons of squires,
Leaving the city and the shires and the seaports,
Eager to establish a temporary home and make a fortune
In the new lands beyond the West, pawning perhaps
The old familiar acres or the assured competence;
Sturdy, realist, eager to wring wealth from these Barbadoes
And to build, trade, colonize, pay homage to their King,
And worship according to the doctrines of the Church of
    England.

I see these ancestors of ours
Torn from the hills and dales of their motherland,
Weeping, hoping in the mercy of time to return
To farm and holding, shuttle and loom, to return
In snow or rain or shine to humble homes, their own;
Cursing the day they were cheated by rebel standards,
Or betrayed for their country's honour; fearing
The unknown land, the fever and the hurricane,
The swamp and jungle – all the travellers' tales.

I see them, these ancestors of ours;
Children of the tribe, ignorant of their doom, innocent
As cattle, bartered for, captured, beaten, penned,
Cattle of the slave-ship, less than cattle;
Sold in the market-place, yoked to servitude;
Cattle, bruised and broken, but strong enough to plough and
    breed,

And promised white man's heaven where they sing,
Fill lamps with oil nor wait the Bridegroom's coming;
Raise chorused voices in the hymn of praise.

(Frank Collymore, Barbados)

And Derek Walcott's declaration, on receiving the Nobel Prize for
Literature, concerning the Caribbean people about whom he writes,
should be closely considered, and never forgotten. Walcott was born
in St Lucia, and grew up there; he attended the University College
of the West Indies at Mona, Jamaica, and established the Trinidad
Theatre Workshop while working there. His declaration states:

> They survived the Middle Passage and the FATE ROZACK,
> the ship that carried the first indentured Indians from the port
> of Madras to the fields of FELICITY [a small village in
> Trinidad] that carried the chained Cromwellian convict and
> the Sephardic Jew, the Chinese grocer and the Lebanese
> merchant selling samples on his bicycle.

Those are the ones of whom Port of Spain reminds Walcott. But in
Omeros he adds many others to these, people who were, and are, all
part of European geopolitics and the European out-push throughout
the whole of the Americas – an out-push that brought together so
many cultures. An out-push which created a culture too rich to be
designated, by European or Caribbean people, as being either black
or white, and too rich to be dealt with simply by matching skin
colour when trying to find and sustain suitable upbringing for those
children who, wherever they were born and wherever they travel,
need the maintenance of family life or fostering and adoption plus
education and opportunity.

Let the poets speak again: first A.L. Hendriks and then John J.
Figueroa:

Madonna of the Unknown Nation*

Caribbean woman!
I watch you
Walking in every land
Of this semi-circled sea.

You are Barbadian mauby-seller
Trinidadian roti-vendor
Puerto Rican cane-reaper
Cuban cigar-roller
Television reporter
Limbo-dancer
Wife of Prime Minister

Wife of Governor
Yourself Minister, Mayor, Senator,
Dungle Queen of the Rasta!

I have watched you
En doudou in Martinique,
In your *gwan wobe* in Guadeloupe,
and wearing your mantilla
In San Jose, Maracaibo, and Barranquilla,
Seen you
Sculptured in the wimple of Sint Maarten nun,

Flagrant in the scents
Of a Haitian prostitute,
Jumping calypso in Port-of-Spain,
Dwelling miserably in Belize tenements:
Career-girl, housewife, unmarried grandmother,
Knotting the society together
With your versatility forever.

Your hands gather fishnets of the past;
Your breasts offer the solaces of now;
Your eyes are deep with the Zion of tomorrow;

Your weeping and your laughter
Are our flutes and our guitars.

Whether you speak Creole or English,
Dutch, French, Spanish,
Or Papiamento; whether you are a Sangmelee,
Half-Chinee,
White, Black, or Coolie,
It does not matter to me:
What is important is that you are holy.

You are emblem of darkness, and emblem of light:
The brave symbol of your body
Reassuring us
Comforting us
Cool shadow of cloud by day
Sweet passion of fire by night.

O Caribbean woman,
I watch you
Walking in every land
Of this semi-circled sea!

And,
Whether I travel to legendary ends of the earth,

Whether I become rich, powerful or famous,
Whether I renounce the world
For poverty and priesthood,
Or the world renounces me
Leaving me ashamed and alone,
However far I go, I will always know this:
It is you inevitably that I must meet,
Caribbean woman!

My pilgrimage then,
Not to Mecca, Jerusalem, or Rome,
But ultimately, with humility, home
To touch with reverence, to wash, to kiss
Your sand-flecked, sea-veined feet.

(A.L. Hendriks, Jamaica)
*'The Caribbean is, unknown to itself, one nation' *The Sunday Times*, London,
1971

'I have a dream'
Columbus Lost or All o' wi a search

The Afrocentric finds great pleasure in
(And laughs assuring self and clientele)
Reminding us that Colon had lost
His way
So stupid was Columbus, lost
European, he called these nightingale
Places the Indies (West)
(Later others finding snakes
In Haiti thought their kindly Gods
Had crossed the seas
Weaving worship of the phallic kind
From Africa.

   The Minoan Goddess, gold
And light, loved serpents too!)

   The man so fool yu si
   Him tink a India him come!

And touring Europeans of the wandering kind
(Some are black and some are white)
Find Africa, neither East nor West,
Just Africa, in these seas.

   But him so fool yu si
   Him tink a India him come.

How easy to travel far
And not arrive at where you are
(Some nowhere finding home)
To escape and not achieve your goal
Is intolerable: India or Africa.

   To search is, or is not
   To find.

    But to build up
    Ourselves by showing
    How foolish others are ...

      (The man so fool yu si
      Him tink a India him come)

The certainties that seem so firm
The Afro-cut, Dashiki and the like,
Eroded by constant winds
That blew before Colon and before you,
Will slush away to sea
In sudden gullies with the steeps
You have not terraced,
With the blessed water from your hills
Soiled, unhusbanded.
Colon, ventured by caravel
   You read, tossed by wind rushes from
   Disturbed persons talking.

The whole heap o' wi
So fool you si, mi chile,
We tink a India wi come
Or Africa
An' all the while
A home wi deh, a home
Yu neber lose yet, nu?

Mek sure a weh you deh
As the man say
Are you ashamed because you're lost
(Laughing at others!) Can you
Forget the fading of the dream
Forget the wavering of the quest
Deep into the unknown
Through tangled forests and empty seas
Amidst amazing currents where
The pointing of the path,
The firmness of the feet, depend

On bursts of bird-song shifting shifting ...

St Thomas/Cidra/Mona (March–May 1972)

(John J. Figueroa, Jamaica)

4 Caribbean achievers

Fed with the same foods, hurt with the same weapons, subject
to the same diseases, healed by the same means ...
(Shakespeare *Merchant of Venice*, Act 3, Scene I)

Despite the problems of migration, of the misunderstandings
between people of differing cultures, and of prejudice, there have
been achievements among the Caribbean heritage (CH) community
which must be taken into account. Some people have done quite well
despite continuing complaints of discrimination in some fields such
as the law. The achievements have not been consistent – yet another
reason for not thinking that simply being black will be a hallmark of
success, or of suitability to foster or adopt. Some of the more public
achievers are known, such as Lord David Pitt in the House of Lords,
and the West Indian heritage persons in the House of Commons. In
broadcasting there are quite a few persons from the group. But sometimes it is not appreciated how many immigrants have become head-
teachers, and done well in business. For this reason a small group of
Caribbean heritage people, mainly in the Midlands, were, with the
help of a grant from the Bustamante Institute of Jamaica, interviewed by John J. Figueroa. Some of the results of that study will
now be stated partly to dispel the view that Caribbean heritage
people are always underachievers, and also to underline the variety

of achievement concerned – and the variety of 'black' people involved.

The first person we will consider is a young woman from Jamaica, who would there have been called Chinese Jamaican. Her father's family has taken an English sounding name, a practice more common in Guyana and Trinidad than in Jamaica. But he reverted to the original Chinese family name. And when she married, in Jamaica, a young Englishman, her maiden name was Chinese. They were teachers and they decided to settle in England. When she got to England with her white husband who was from Lancashire she found that she was not white despite her husband, nor Chinese despite her looks, but black. (One is reminded that in apartheid South Africa Chinese were declared black, Japanese white – a wonderful example of the fact that if you have money 'you takes your choice'.)

She had been teaching in a Catholic school when she met her husband; he had come out to Jamaica on a teaching contract early in the 1970s. The fact that she was a Catholic helped her to settle in with her in-laws, and in the community which was heavily Catholic.

We will give the interview with her in some detail, as it illustrates many points that are relevant to our discussion. In the case of other achievers interviewed we will refer only to points of interest. None of them had an interview of less time or detail than the one with the lady in question, whom we shall call J.S.:

> J.S.: I got a job straight away but I suppose I got a job because the applications went in through my husband's family. They were able to point me in the right direction, but I didn't have any problems having my teacher's qualifications recognised. I'd been trained at the University of the West Indies and was given a DES number without any difficulty and went straight into teaching. I arrived in July (in the mid-1970s) and began teaching in September. I taught in what had very recently been a secondary modern school, so it was generally considered quite a rough school. I found it very, very tough, I found it very different and I didn't so much find anything that would openly be called prejudice, but I certainly found people ignorant and asking odd questions about where I had come from and my background and so on.

> J.F.: Were there any children from the Caribbean, or of Caribbean heritage, in your school?

> J.S.: There was one family and they had two children in the school and I had one occasion when I taught the girl. I was covering a class for her regular teacher. But they were not

anxious to be pointed out as different. They were very settled and successful in the area. The children did extremely well at school and although I said once or twice to her 'you know I would love to meet your father and talk about home' it was never followed up, and I just took it that they didn't particularly want to be singled out as being different. And the children themselves were successful in the school, they didn't seem to be having any difficulty and they were certainly doing very well academically.

I found it a very interesting experience because I suppose I wasn't aware that I had only taught in very good schools, in Jamaica. In a sense schools with very high standards and discipline. So I had not really taught a rough class before. So I was dealing with that which was new to me as a teacher and I was also dealing with adjusting to being in Preston which is where we went. It was a good experience in the end because I learnt a lot from those children about being Lancashire children – and they were working class. Very outspoken, quite tough, but very responsive and communicative and I think we learnt a lot from each other in the time I was there.

What I found was that they didn't know much about the Caribbean. They had this idea in their heads that it was very primitive, that we didn't live in houses. They were fascinated by things like my hair and they asked me all sorts of odd questions about whether we had such and such a thing in the Caribbean. Eventually I took a photo album in and showed them pictures of, you know, my family's home, the kinds of friends we had and so on. And they were very surprised at the buildings in the pictures and they were also very surprised at the racial mix of the people in the pictures that I took to them.

It is funny how moving away puts your own experience into perspective. Because it hadn't struck me that it was remarkable that I had friends from all kinds of racial groups until they were so surprised to see the mix in the pictures.

Because being quite light in colour, in Jamaica I wouldn't really be regarded as black. And I was increasingly surprised by the assumptions people made about that, and by just a generally patronising attitude. And their wanting to explain quite obvious things to me and tell me how certain things were done when, you know, I was perfectly accustomed to those things and knew what they were like.

So I think my first year here was ... I found it difficult because I felt so out of place – but not out of place because anybody was very hostile to me; out of place because I had come from a very different place in Jamaica: you know everybody knew me, my family. I was accustomed to people knowing who I was. And I came here and I was Tony's wife and that was it, and I think that was what I found hardest of all.

After we left Preston we went to live in Bolton. My husband got a job in Manchester and Bolton was kind of half way between family and the job. And again that was very different because I began to work with the second language teaching programme there and did quite a lot of work with the Asian community in Bolton. And seeing the kinds of response that they met, and how they dealt with it, as well as the whole business of not speaking English and how that affected how people responded to you.

I was working with Asian families mainly because we were doing the programme to teach English to women especially who weren't able to go out to training schemes or to schools and so on.

So I think that began to open my eyes to how England saw people who weren't white, and I found that the language thing was a great confusion. That the thing that people picked on when they made statements about Asians that were negative was they talked about their 'gibberish' and how they couldn't understand what they were saying and so on. And I began to have some idea of how English people saw people who were different.

But really I think the turning point for me was I was at home with two young children and I was anxious to make some links, I felt so isolated living in Bolton, and there was a summer job advertised in the Manchester Teachers' Paper for a part-time teacher to do literacy work. Just for the summer on a summer school and it was in Moss Side which of course is a Caribbean area in Manchester. And my husband was a teacher so he was able to be home for the summer. So he took on the kids, and he said 'right, OK, off you go, go and do something different'. And I worked for three weeks at Ducie Central where they had based the adult literacy school, and that was a real eye opener.

J.F.: I can imagine. You know I also taught at Ducie Central.

J.S.: Yes, there we are. Now the thing about that is that first of all I was the first 'black' teacher in the literacy programme and yet almost all the students, not all but certainly over 50 per cent of the students were from a Caribbean background, and they were in the vast majority Jamaican. So that was lovely for me because here were people who understood where I was coming from, who knew a lot about my background, who could find ...

you know make guesses about me because they knew the kind of culture I came from. But also it was such a revelation to the white teachers that there were Jamaican people who were on the other side of the desk.

And it was a huge boost for the students that they were being taught by somebody black and that teacher was also teaching the white students. So you know that really just convinced me that I had to find a way to get a bit closer to this kind of community because I felt that when I was in Preston I was anonymous. And what I thought were my special skills were irrelevant. I felt in Manchester they were very relevant and I could make some links and begin to feel at home.

J.F.: Let me put to you a really embarrassing and puzzling question. Do you think that you have been helped with both the Jamaican or Caribbean people, most of whom are Jamaican, and the English, because you aren't all that black?

J.S.: Yes, absolutely, absolutely. In fact it's a very complicated thing because I found often people would be quite anti to me because they would assume that you know, I must be one of those high-brown 'facety' [superior, self-regarding] women who wouldn't want to know them. And one of the things that saved my skin was that I could speak really good patois ... And so ... you know like throw out this line that I'm identifying, and I'm happy to be Jamaican.

I'm very Jamaican by using patois, and often that was quite a turning point in people's attitude towards me. In fact it is interesting that the woman who is now working with me, when she first met me she said that she decided she wasn't going to have anything to do with me because I was definitely a high-brown middle class woman from Jamaica and I wouldn't be interested in ordinary people. So yes definitely. It had a two-way effect.

It's such an assumption here that Caribbean people are all black and in fact the expression Afro-Caribbean has become completely accepted because it's kind of assumed if people are Caribbean they must be black. And in general English people expect that if you are Caribbean you are going to be black and they will be taken aback and they can't quite make out where you are coming from if you are Caribbean and not black.

And I think it is a mistake in a way because it blurs the fact that the Caribbean is culturally all mixed. I know the whites would certainly accept that the predominant Caribbean identity is black, and certainly although my background is very Chinese it is also very Afro in culture. I mean my whole orientation is certainly more Afro than Chinese. But it's just that people make blind assumptions that all Jamaicans are black.

J.F.: Yes but also there must be very few other places in the world in which somebody can say my culture is partly African and partly Chinese. And that is what I think that some of the Jamaicans, I shouldn't say Jamaicans, Jamaican heritage people here are losing sight of: they are asking the British, quite rightly, to be multicultural. But at the same time they are tending to forget they come from a multicultural situation. And in coming from a multicultural situation they should put this forward to the English.

J.S.: I think that there is still a lot of institutional things operating against the children who come from the Caribbean background. In the sense that a lot of things about schools and exams and so on, especially language are real barriers to their getting on well in schools.

I think that is increasingly being recognised but whether there is still any will to do anything about changing those factors, I am beginning to doubt; and I am beginning to feel that a small number of black people are succeeding and doing well and going through and are going to be you know, very successful and do well. But I think that they are going to be a very narrow top of a steep pyramid.

Because it seems to me that in most black families the children are not doing well enough in schools to guarantee them success in what is becoming increasingly a meritocratic way of doing things. And so I think that the outlook for us generally is quite bleak. I think that we are going to remain in low paid, low status jobs. But I think there is going to be a growing black middle class and hopefully you know, that will make for some change.

J.F.: Yesterday at my lecture a senior English teacher responded to my point that the schools in the UK can never be better for 'minorities' until they become better schools for all, in a worrying and pessimistic way.

He said 'what worries me about English schools is that they seem to have lost curiosity'. He continued 'now I teach in a mainly … in a completely white school and what really worries me is that these children don't really have any curiosity about anything in the outside world'.

Such an attitude is bound to have its effect on Caribbean heritage people and on the education of their children. And it is having a devastating influence on the education and general cultural atmosphere of the whole of the United Kingdom. A well known politician was saying on the TV recently that he could see no reason for 'tax payers' to support the Royal Shakespeare Company's productions as that money did not also subsidise the Bingo Halls in his constituency.

Thank you J.S., and more power to your work!

We will return to some of the points made by J.S. in her interview. Before going on may we pose the question of what would be the politically correct solution if J.S.'s children at any time needed fostering or adoption. Should they be restricted to a black family since their mother was 'black', or a Chinese family since she looks Chinese (the children look white). Should a cousin of their father be barred from fostering or adopting them since he is white and the children black?

Those who met J.S. in the UK were surprised that so-called 'black English' (Jamaican Creole) is not spoken only by people of African ancestry, a fact first recorded in the early nineteenth century. To this day Creole is spoken by blonde farmers, Chinese, Indians and by every combination of these as well as by people with black skins.

The Caribbean heritage community, like other minority and 'disadvantaged' groups, seems to progress in waves. One of the interviewees, a distinguished West Indian diplomat, and former RAF officer, twice decorated, stresses the ready acceptability which the migrants met at first, not necessarily in matters of housing. But certainly they were sought after as workers.

And I can remember, in about 1948, when a bus driver passed a stop before some black men, in RAF uniform, could stop the bus, that an old lady, supported by her fellow passengers, read the riot act to the driver – although it was not clear that he had passed them 'on ethnic grounds'. His contention was that it was a request stop and that they had not signalled. Her reply was 'You very well know, duckie, that they don't know that they are supposed to signal.'

There can be no doubt that at one stage CH people were sought after, and encouraged to come to the UK. But then the attitude changed. Was this because of a 'backlash', or of economic decline, or of racism, or of xenophobia, or of the increased migration? It is difficult to think of UK hospitals without nurses from the CH community, and of London Transport without West Indian conductors and drivers. Many of these people were recruited well before they got to the UK.

Although it is not a popular thing to say – it is almost totally taboo! – one simply has to raise the question of to what extent the breaking up and division of homes has contributed to some of the problems of CH people in the UK. It must not be thought that this breaking up is only a 'working class problem'. One male interviewee, of middle class origins, spoke with deep feeling about coming over, as a boy of about eleven, to a father he did not know, who insisted that he did not wander about one of the tougher city streets as he was accustomed to in the countryside of Jamaica. It took him years to realise that the father he did not know was not merely taking it out on him for appearing in England. And he was able after hard study to become a successful businessman.

Some interviewees have spoken of the trauma of finding, on coming to England, that their biological father had disappeared, and someone else had taken his place in their mother's affections. Of course there are progressive people who, coming out of a fairly stable background as far as class, culture, language and finance go, will tell you that it does not make any difference whether the father a child finds is the biological parent or not. But such people are likely to have little experience of the possible trauma of not finding the father or mother one knew, when this experience is added to the shocks of climate and culture as well as those of adolescence. So that fostering which arises either directly or indirectly from the trauma of difficult migration cannot bind itself to any simple rule of thumb such as 'matching colours'.

> J.F.: I remember watching a group of 'indigenous' English people – in fact many of them were probably of Irish heritage – as they reacted with fear, disbelief and real anxiety to a group of six large CH men who were having a slight argument over the question of whether they were British or West Indian. Three of the young men were saying that they were British, and did not really care about the West Indies and Caribbean matters. The others were maintaining that they were not British but West Indian.
>
> I would have guessed from their speech and accents that they were all born in and around Manchester. But their decibel count, and their gestures, in what was clearly to them a routine and unheated conversation, conveyed to all around them at the cafeteria tables the clear sign that at any minute 'violence was going to break out'. The group had no feeling for what in fact they were communicating to the other people in the cafeteria, and the non-CH people present had very little insight into the fact that they were all the while interpreting gestures, sounds, noise according to their own accustomed cultural norms.

This kind of cross cultural mis-signalling is common. But few people seem to acknowledge it, or take it into account when considering the situation of minorities in this country, nor in the interpretation which the 'native' British are likely to give to the habits of 'immigrants', and to their suitability to adopt or foster.

Let us return now to some of the points raised by the 'Chinese Jamaican' lady. First of all she is an achiever, and was in charge of many important educational enterprises in the Manchester area. She is now a top officer in the Midlands processing entry to Access type courses leading to higher education and helping to design such courses for adults who have not done well at the secondary level of schooling.

But she clearly had the support of her Lancastrian husband and his family. Even then she had to prove to many that in Jamaica she had actually lived in a house. By the questions put to her she came to realise how England saw people who were not 'white'. It is truly amazing how a culture which ran one of the biggest empires ever known to man can be so ignorant of the outside world, especially of former colonies and their peoples. Two other points are relevant to the culture in which decisions about fostering and adoption and education will take place and be directed. As she puts it:

> In general English people expect that if you are Caribbean you are going to be black and they will be taken aback and they can't quite make out where you are coming from if you are Caribbean and not black ... [and]

> ... a small number of black people [in the UK] are succeeding and doing well and going through and are going to be you know, very successful and do well. But I think they are going to be a very narrow top of a steep pyramid.

Note the very steep pyramid. England, particularly, is a libertarian society; but it most certainly is not an egalitarian one. Were it, some parents would not be paying £10,000+ to send a child to 'public school'. Not only is the education in such schools supposed to be better, but one's children are kept away from the wrong sort, and have every opportunity to build up connections and networks which will be of immense value for the rest of their lives (note the Tizard and Phoenix (1993) study discussed in Chapter 6). Despite all the talk of sportsmanship there are very few 'level playing fields' in English society: the wrong accent, the wrong tie, may sink you, or so it is thought.

So the steep pyramid does not face only immigrants, but all of society. It is highly unlikely that 'minorities' will get better schooling until the whole system is improved.

It is no doubt an awareness of these complications and difficulties which have moved caring people to look for best solutions when children already 'disadvantaged' (by being 'black' or different) have to be fostered or adopted. But the situation is too complicated to be much helped by painting by numbers.

We will look in less detail at the experience of other achievers who were interviewed. One interviewee, a Jewish young man, who had worked in Jamaica and is connected by marriage to the Caribbean heritage group had a few interesting points to make:

> My first main contact with Caribbean heritage children was actually in Jamaica; and when I came back and taught in England I was so struck by the difference in attitude between the black children of Caribbean heritage in London, whom I was teaching. They were so negative, and difficult at school compared to the same age children that I'd been teaching in Jamaica.
>
> I became convinced that there had to be some difference in the society and in the schools rather than seeing that kind of performance and behaviour as something internal to the children. And that's why, that's how I got involved in multicultural education in 1978 ...
>
> And yes there are plenty of successes. I think that there's a slight danger a lot of those successes come in ways that people see as stereotypical. There is a tradition for people to succeed in sport when economically there may be an avenue for success, and that would be true for all different kinds of races. In the 1930s there was a traditional means of improvement for Jews in the East End [of London], there were lots of Jewish boxers.
>
> No one really said anything about that being due to genetic or racial differences. They may be inclined to say that more in terms of black fighters now being successful. But within sports there's certainly been an explosion of black talent and I think it's interesting to speculate why that is ... within the 1970s you went from a position of being almost no top British footballers who were black to a situation within ten years where most clubs in the first division would have one or two or three black players. And it couldn't be seen that simply black players started getting better, it had to be seen in terms of clubs' attitudes and willingness to go out and look for them ...
>
> It's really interesting when you look at different sports and see that some of them have top black stars, table tennis but not tennis, and it would be very strange if the abilities were confined to those sports where black players have succeeded ...

We will now look briefly at the experience of some other inter- viewees to see what light their struggle to achieve throws on the complicated pattern of Caribbean experience in Britain. Of course the young people or infants now in school, or likely to need fostering or adoption will be a generation, at least, after the interviewees but will be taught by or placed with people who are likely to be the contemporaries of the interviewees, who also may act as role models for Caribbean heritage children.

There used to be a feeling that a child who had started school in the Caribbean and then come over to continue his schooling would usually do better than those CH children born here. But of two of the outstanding persons interviewed, both of whom have gone to the top of their professions, one came over after a few years of secondary school in Jamaica, one was born here of Jamaican parents.

What was behind the assumptions referred to, was the feeling that the Caribbean heritage child born here would not only be subjected to general racism but, in school, to low expectation of his abilities to perform or stereotypic ways of looking at his potential. Such experiences would have held him/her up, even perhaps resulting in alienation from the whole of school activities. There is some general basis for this assumption, but it is too wide an assumption, and does not take into account the possibility of countervailing factors such as the family and the specific character of the child concerned.

One of the interviewees (G.B.) who was born here, and who is now in charge of a junior school (with an attached nursery section) claims that the greatest factor in his doing well in the school system, and in his going through teachers' college courses, and getting a school to run at a fairly young age, was his father and the religious faith of his family. He says in part:

> I was born in Wolverhampton in 1953, which is just up the road from here. The training I had in fact was the standard training. The teacher's training itself, at that time it was a 3-year training programme which I actually did about 13 years ago. As far as my background is concerned my parents were always very ambitious and supportive. Ambitious and supportive because as well as having the desire for me to attain certain high goals they were well aware that there was a certain amount of work that had to be done in between in order for me to reach that stage. They were very, very encouraging, still are very encouraging to this day and always saw whatever achievement I made as a step in the right direction. I was never made to feel complacent … but I was to look further.

> J.F.: Can you think of any people who acted as it were as kind of examples to you?

> G.B.: I think the one that springs first and foremost to mind is

my father. My father, very proud man, very dignified man, a person who believed in the individual trying to excel themselves. As I said before he came from very humble beginnings, he's a minister in Wolverhampton and he plays a very prominent part in community affairs within the region itself and he has always believed that an individual should never see themself as ever finishing their course, that there's always a further step to go and he's been very encouraging to me in that respect.

One knows that no one factor brings about success, but he attributes much of his to a really stable and encouraging family background.

True it is that he is an outstanding person, not only hardworking but having a wonderful way of relating to people. His parents were black Jamaicans; his school population is:

> ... predominantly Asian, by that I am saying that at least 55 per cent are children who originate from the Indian subcontinent. We have amongst that group Sikhs, Hindus, Muslims approximately in equal number of the three major groups. We do have small numbers of children who are Buddhists, we also have a small number of children who are Indian or Asian Christians. We have a small Vietnamese population within the Asian Christians who are of the Catholic religion ... 20 per cent is Afro-Caribbean who you would say are either Church of England, or Pentecostal. We have one or two children from the Afro-Caribbean group who have Rastafarian leanings. And then the remaining smaller group, very small but it is steadily increasing, we have indigenous whites who are either Church of England or of no particular religion.

There are about six major languages among the pupils.

One goes into all this detail to stress how complicated is the situation, and how complex are the people who are designated as 'black'.

The relation of the school with the community is good; parents know what the school is aiming at, and are sometimes called upon to explain how the languages which they speak differ from other languages spoken as a mother tongue by children in the school.

The most impressive thing about this man's achievement is that he has worked long and hard to attain it. Would a person like this be suitable to adopt, or foster or teach only 'black' children? Or only Caribbean heritage children?

Another one of the interviewees, A.B., has gone quite far, being now a county councillor in one of the biggest conurbations in Great Britain. But his experience differs considerably from the headteacher described above. He was born in Jamaica of black parents. He attributes much to the fact that he went to secondary school in Jamaica. He is full of praise for that school, not particularly on academic grounds. His point is that as a black boy in that school he was in no way made to feel inferior on grounds of colour, nor was he expected not to do as well, in say algebra and geography, as any Chinese or white or brown boys in his class.

He came to England and went to a secondary school in London. He was quite surprised, on leaving that school, to find out that he was thought to have been very confident of his abilities, and ready to ask sensible questions. He on the other hand had thought that he was a bit diffident. He is grateful to the Jamaican school which developed in him that unconscious belief in himself and his abilities, so that he asked for no quarter and gave none.

> J.F.: A colleague in Manchester, on receiving complaints that Caribbean heritage children regularly were up to one hour late for lessons excused this by saying that this was usual and acceptable within their culture.

Note the difference between this attitude and that of young adults who experienced schooling in Jamaica at first hand.

When Caribbean heritage people seek school and teacher improvement only on the grounds of curing racism and improving their lot, the implications are insufficiently recognised. The argument about black role models and apparent non-performance of children in some schools, though important, as indicated above, may get in the way of serious discussion about a means of helping Caribbean heritage people fulfil themselves. While some CH people did well in school, as indicated by these achievers, it would not be right to suppose that all education in the Caribbean was wonderful (this would link with other myths, discussed elsewhere in this book, about the nature of home life in the West Indies). The reality is that, though some education has been very good with discipline and high behavioural standards, there is a two-tier system which has existed and to some extent still does with high percentages of illiteracy throughout the Caribbean other than in Barbados. Caribbean schools also suffer from overcrowding, lack of books and lack of attendance. The education system could slide from being disciplined to being authoritarian, just as can happen in family life between parents and adolescents.

Many Caribbean heritage people have rather overblown expectations of education, understandably so because of the difficult situation in which many parents found themselves. So that they must have longed for an authoritarian wand in the hand of the teacher which could at least make sure that their children would go straight and gain the benefits of living in the UK.

Education, economic power and political power go hand in hand. Whereas many of the interviewees felt that until CH people gained more economic power they would find it harder and harder to climb up the steep pyramid of UK society, the county councillor considers that political power is even more important than economic. He cites the experience of German Jews many of whom had done well economically but who had no kind of political power to save themselves from the savagery of Nazism. But then what group did? (Another indication that a just society should protect all its members.)

After his London schooling, A.B. went on to university, and is well read in philosophy, not least of all in Wittgenstein. He has married a highly educated Irish lady. They have a family of three children. Would they be automatically debarred from adopting, or fostering, or teaching white children?

Another person, a woman this time, who has gone far up the ladder in the field of education, also started her secondary education in Jamaica. After being in charge of the religious department of a secondary school, in the Midlands she became an assistant headteacher, and then an HMI (inspector of schools). She is now in charge of a big secondary school in the Midlands ...

> I was born in Jamaica, went to school up to age 13. Went to Manchester High, Jamaica, my Head at the time being Gerry Jerman. Came here, in fact the funny thing is I actually took the then 11-plus exams. I took it at age 10 and passed, age 11 and passed and went to Manchester High School. Came here and went to an ordinary secondary modern girls' school where the emphasis was certainly not on science at all and we were only expected to do 5 CSEs and nothing more. And I did 6 CSEs and came out with some good grades, twos and ones. Went on after that to do O levels and A levels to sixth form college. Uhm, English, maths, physics, history, social studies and A levels in religious education and English. Then I went on to a college of education ... and did 4 years there. Came out with a 2.2 in education and religious education ...
>
> I think that perhaps I should start with the church in terms of achievement. I belong to one of the Pentecostal churches and I think there I actually see the basis for achievement at that sort of religious cultural level in terms of ..., the churches for a long time over 30 years provided thousands of Afro-Caribbean people with security ...
>
> I actually believe that we need to be appealing more to our youth rather than to many of us because therein lies our future.

And I think in order to do that we have to sit down and actually listen very carefully to what our youth is saying. And not only listen to what they are saying but see where they are at in their thinking, what they do with their spare time, where do they hang out and what, if anything, do we as black people have to challenge our youth or to focus their attention on.

There are very many more black people who are achieving in the business world, in industry, in education, in medicine and so on. But I think always the position is at what – the question I ask myself – is at what cost? Because some of us when we get to where we get to actually either forget where we are coming from, forget our links with our own communities and try to live, or are forced to live, I don't know which one it is, very separate and separated lives ...

This lady has certainly not forgotten 'where she has come from'. In a way, although I doubt that she would forgive one for saying it, she sometimes appears to forget how much she is influenced by British culture, and by the system in which she does such excellent work. Unlike the county councillor she thinks that economic effort and development are essential for the Caribbean heritage community. Like him she knows that confidence is central. But she stresses how that confidence can be built up by membership in small Pentecostal (black) churches.

Our next interviewee came to England from Barbados as a lad. He had been to a good secondary school there and found England disappointing – after all the talk, at home, of going to the mother country. He is also the person, already referred to, who found his father's rules to keep him from the racism of the street rather trying. As one who, within reason, had roamed the streets of tiny Barbados, it took him a long time to realise what his father was protecting him from.

He tends to agree with those who feel that improved economic effort and status is what Caribbean heritage people need:

I feel that up to now we have used a lot ... we have spent a lot of our energies and time in terms of fighting a political battle but you know I think that if you're doing that from a position of weakness then all you'd be doing is making a lot of noise and you wouldn't make any progress. I would like to see the Caribbean heritage people putting their own house in order and building up an economic base from which they can lever important things. Important concessions from the society which has actually become our home whether we like it or not ...

[As he says]

> I am the Coordinator of Handsworth Employment Scheme Limited. I've been founder member and first employee of this community organisation which started in 1979. But before that I did a number of things ...
>
> I did my studies and went on to train as a teacher because I always saw that as my vocation. After that I was teaching at a secondary school in Birmingham at a place called Northfields which is a majority white area and I was a teacher of mathematics there for a couple of years. And there were a number of teachers who had taught in Handsworth who actually moved over to Northfields and I would sit in the staff room and I would hear them talking about working in schools in Handsworth. The image of black kids that they were portraying was one of youngsters who were not at all interested in education and I couldn't understand this because my whole experience in the Caribbean was of youngsters always hungry for education. Youngsters willing to walk 10 miles to school every day for education.

He is not the first person to note this difference in attitude to school between Caribbean people at home and those who grow up in the UK. What really is the basis of this difference which in turn helps people to believe that 'Caribbean people are not up to much' ... despite the evidence of the achievements of some of them?

He goes on:

> I came to take up this post at the William Murdoch School in Handsworth in 1971 and I got my first introduction to race relations in Britain because up to then between 1963 and 1971 ... I lived such a sheltered life. My parents made sure I wasn't exposed to racism as such. Anyway I got to know some youngsters who all their lives had lived in a situation of racial discrimination, who had actually grown up on the underbelly of the society and who had seen things in the raw and they were fairly bitter about the kind of society they were living in.

He and some colleagues helped to introduce what one might generally call black studies:

> The headmaster saw this as undermining his authority. He brought in the chief education officer and they carried out an investigation, they decided that what we were teaching the youngsters was 'black power' and they decided to close down the department and we had to look for alternative employment ...

[So I decided]

... to do a PhD at the University of Warwick. The area of research was the growth of the corporate black identity, which I completed in about 1981.

I was from 1976 a lecturer at a teacher's training college in Dudley. I did that for a year, then after that I was a research worker at the University of Aston in the Management Centre where I wrote a paper on the decline of the inner city ...

Even though the causes of the decline of the inner city are many [I came to believe] ... that one of the things that actually compounds the plight of blacks is the tendency for successful blacks to flee the inner city. And I made the decision to come back and make a contribution ...

There are a lot of people who argue that the society is incorrigibly racist, that is ingrained in the culture and in the structure of the society, and that the best thing an aware person could do is to resist and, to use the jargon, to undermine the foundations of Babylon. I think that it is very foolish you know, because you can bring down the edifice around your own ears.

So he tries to persuade 'blacks' that many of them have to face the fact that the UK is now their home, and that they have to work to make it a better home. Note that he feels strongly that the 'inner city' loses its better people. It's hard to see what one does about that. A promising ballet dancer growing up in, say, Bradford would certainly have to move to London (or Paris or New York) if he/she wished to go far in dance, but inner cities nevertheless need not be home only to the currently disadvantaged.

Notice that he, and many others, have left teaching, where they are no doubt much needed: they have left for administrative posts or for other fields. One of the most interesting of the interviewees who has become head of a large important secondary school in the Midlands, which has recently gone out on its own, mused while he was being interviewed that he had recommended his students to become engineers, doctors, lawyers, but never teachers. This underlines a general problem of the society: the downgrading of the teaching profession. Its preparation is woefully inadequate, and a non-interventionist government has felt it necessary to impugn its professional status by telling it exactly what it must teach – with a minimum of consultation. Here again we have an example of the fact that there can be little improvement for minority groups, whether in education or social services, until the systems are improved for the whole of society – until the workers in these important fields are given a fuller preparation for their difficult tasks and not just provided with simple minded politically correct solutions.

It is also clear that strong family ties, availability of schools whose teachers are regarded as professionals who in turn expect and value achievement, as well as help from religious groups, have given many of the Caribbean heritage people who have achieved confidence and self-belief. Circumstances which encourage this quality should be sought on behalf of all children including those from minority groups, should be made available to them by parents, the wider community, social services for children in need and through educational opportunity.

5 United Kingdom/ West Indies: family life, health and education

From the Caribbean with Love

We seek no enemy abroad
But as all must
Watch the enemy within
The certainty of ignorance
The large claims of smallness
The desire to be master
Or slave
The temptations to forget too little
Or to remember too much
To imitate those we
Say we do not honour
So as to prove what needs no proof
That we are God's children
As free and as bound
As all our brothers.

John J. Figueroa (1992)

When the Caribbean came to the motherland in the 1950s and 1960s 60 per cent of the immigrants were Jamaican. These are not the only influences however. In Bradford are to be found citizens

and descendants of St Lucia and St Vincent whose religion is
Catholic and whose creole is French. London Transport in the
1950s actively recruited in Barbados with the support of the Barbadian government. Suddenly, it seemed, many young black bus conductors and drivers worked on the London buses and underground
system. The Caribbean was one in the sense that traders moved
between the islands (John J. Figueroa was greeted in Martinique by
a man from St Vincent selling fresh vegetables from his launch) but
in the main people remained in their 'born-island' and travelled
little until they sought financial security far from their homes.

At that time Jamaican currency had parity with American and
people of wealth, academics and businessmen could afford to travel
either to the USA or the UK. This however was the first time that
descendants of those who made the middle passage to the Caribbean
had travelled of their own choice, as emigrants. It was the wage earn-
ers who left.

James (1994) writes of a 'new pan-Caribbean consciousness'
which, he says, is hard to find since the islands of the Caribbean are
scattered within a seascape. Port of Spain in Trinidad is more than
a thousand miles from Kingston, Jamaica. At the time of mass emi-
gration, transport between the islands was expensive, scanty and
rarely used. Travel within and between the islands of the Caribbean
was a rarity other than for merchants, writers and occasional
tourists. A Jamaican living in Brooklyn or Notting Hill, even today,
is more likely to meet Barbadians and Trinidadians than is his coun-
tryman living in Montego Bay. For James, the new Caribbean consciousness is that belonging to a student in the City University of
New York, who can meet and become friends with emigrants from
Barbados to the Bahamas.

Back at home the matriarchal tradition, defined by many as
being rooted in a slave culture when only mothers and children had
any chance of staying together and males were valued as workers,
not as fathers of families, meant that a family network was available
to care for the left-behind children. Commonly, grandmothers took
on the task. Thus, the break up of family networks, described in the
previous chapters, did not deprive the little ones in the West Indies
of care from an extended family, especially in the rural areas.

The effects were seen in English cities, when young children
were born to recently settled parents who had to work long hours
and who, like other immigrants before them, were less favoured in
their access to housing.

A child of two years, whose father worked on London Transport
and whose mother was a hospital orderly, did not have access to the
yard, no grandmother, no aunts, no network of children, no traffic-
free place in which to play. Childminders were available but money

to pay them was small and there was still
play materials. So the child who in the
suffered a parasite infection, an inadequate
health care but who received affection and
now might spend many hours in a small
nity to talk or explore, although with bette
family budget for food.

In the late 1960s a phrase, 'West Indi
rency. It was racist, since it attributed to a particular culture a problem common to all children who are under-stimulated; that they are
expressionless, unresponsive even when attempts are made to stim-
ulate them, delayed in speech and motor skills and may end up stim-
ulating themselves by repetitive behaviours such as rocking. Thus,
newly arrived families on limited incomes, unfamiliar with local
resources and preoccupied by long hours of work, inadvertently created a situation where, as would happen with any small child, there
was a falling back in development of those deprived of opportunities
for talk, play and exploration.

In the early seventies many Inner London schools started 'nurture groups' (Boxall 1976). These were invaluable and deceptively
simple arrangements whereby young children who for whatever
reason, and irrespective of their nationality or skin colour, were
unprepared to cope with pre-school and primary school, were lov-
ingly and systematically taught the skills to care for themselves, the
language to communicate with other children and enabled to play.
The results were invaluable to the children, their teachers and their
parents and it is sad to record that, because so many small black children joined these groups, the provision in the end was labelled as
racist. This was the view of some educationists, including those of
the same skin colour as the children, but not of the parents who
valued what was being offered and could see how their children
benefited. The children lost out, whatever their skin colour.

The second wave of trouble came as older children, brought up
by extended families, came to England to join their emigrant parent
or parents. Commonly this happened as adolescence approached.
Typically, a twelve year old boy or girl would be sent to the mother
country by a grandmother now in her fifth or sixth decade. Home
would now be with a mother or father who had married and pro-
duced a new family of younger children. School would be a 1970s
comprehensive, often with 1,000 or more pupils, the language substantially different from the native creole. Disproportionate numbers of children from the Caribbean fell behind with schoolwork; it
was often unclear to teachers whether the boy or girl was showing a
specific delay in reading or mathematics or whether the underlying
problem was 'limited ability'. There was little time or resource for

...ding the lives of those who had uprooted themselves and ...f training and skills tailored to the teachers who took on ... unfamiliar problems which may, therefore, have been exaggerated or avoided.

Thus 'black' children were referred, in numbers disproportionate to those within the community, to special education services. They showed up on records of poor attendance and bad behaviour and many, particularly the boys, were at risk of being suspended. There were knock-on effects in their involvement with juvenile justice systems.

It is easier to notice, particularly when they stand out because of their skin colour, children who are failing, behaving badly or truanting. By comparison, successes are unsung apart from a few records, such as those made by John J. Figueroa and described in Chapter 4, of specific enquiry into achievement and triumph over adversity. Resilience and courage in adversity are less obvious than trouble and continuing disadvantage.

Nurture groups disappeared for the wrong reasons such as racial prejudice and lack of resources. Specifically in relation to the Caribbean diaspora, the need lessened as families achieved better housing, re-established social networks and learned to make use of primary health care, school and childcare. Yet nurture groups can be valuable to any child whose family is in trouble and should be available as part of any comprehensive education service as should small, specialist teaching groups for older children with problems of behaviour and learning, particularly the acquisition of linguistic skills.

Black (1985) writes of Caribbean children:

> On starting school the children suffered disadvantages in language and, later, in verbal and non-verbal reasoning and reading skills; these disadvantages tended to persist throughout their school career and afterwards, when they started to look for jobs.
>
> The present generation of Afro-Caribbean children entering primary school, however, have no language problems if they have attended a nursery school and are also more likely to have a stable home and to be looked after by their parents in the pre-school years; their progress in primary school is now indistinguishable from that of other groups.

Health

There have been other problems too. Rastafarians, for example, are strict vegetarians (eating only vegetables and no animal products). If the diet is closely observed and income is limited children may develop nutritional deficiences. For example, rickets, which had all but disappeared in the UK, was observed sometimes in children whose diet was restricted and who had lost the sunlight of their native land. Nutritional advice and adequate income overcome such difficulties. In general though, Afro-Caribbean children in the UK, with the one exception described below, are no more prone to illness or disease than is the indigenous population and should be given the same health care, wherever they may live.

In sickle cell disease red blood cells contain abnormal haemoglobin which causes them to form a sickle shape when exposed to low oxygen tension. Outside Africa the distribution corresponds to that of people who were dispersed by the slave trade to the West Indies and America though it is also found in the population around the Persian Gulf and in some parts of India (probably carried there by the armies of Alexander the Great (Lobo 1978)).

If children carry sickle cell trait there are no symptoms but it is important that parents know their child is a carrier and that young people themselves are counselled before they become parents. The condition itself, which occurs when two parents, each with the trait, produce an affected child, is a serious matter. The sickle cells have a short life and are fragile so that sufferers are anaemic, with an enlarged spleen which works to replace damaged blood cells and possible liver damage as that organ works overtime to clear waste products from the breakdown of damaged cells. Babies may fail to thrive, with recurrent infections, haemolytic jaundice and the enlarged spleen gradually shrinks as it becomes damaged.

Older children are particularly liable to recurrent infections and there may be severe 'sickling crises' when blood cells break down in large numbers in response to infections, traumas, cold or anaesthetics. Sometimes there are local swellings of hands or feet because small blood vessels have become blocked (Department of Health Standing Advisory Comittee 1994).

Specialised dental care, regular check ups, advanced intensive treatment of infections and sometimes blood transfusions are necessary. The anxieties are such that a Sickle Cell Society has been formed. It is ironic that the sickle cell trait exists alongside the genetic traits which protect against malarial infection. It seems to have survived within populations because of this beneficent effect yet the diaspora to the United States, the Caribbean and then to the UK has left a situation in which genetic disadvantage outweighs advantage.

The Sickle Cell Society, first set up in Brent in 1979, has made recommendations of services which include:

— funding via national and local health education units for information leaflets;
— better training for medical and nursing staff about sickle cell disease and other haemoglobinopathies both in basic and in-service training;
— a screening policy for newborn babies;
— patients with inherited illnesses such as SCD should be exempt from prescription charges;
— they should be allocated funds for research and that the Department of Health should take an active role in promoting these recommendations.

Anionwu (1993) comments that there is still a long way to go in achieving these basic aims.

In Birmingham, in the 1960s, some black communities resented and resisted assessment of risk for sickle cell disease, claiming that investigation was a form of racism. Today a wise Afro-Caribbean community regards screening, genetic counselling, effective prophylactic care and mutual support for families as a necessity relevant to their specific heritage.

There are other minor conditions which occur more commonly in Afro-Caribbean children. Black (1985) lists:

— Umbilical hernia which may persist until three or four years of age and on occasion may require operation.
— Keloid formation: white coloured, hard, expanded repair tissue is more likely to develop in post-operative scars after burns or injuries than in other racial groups.
— Nutritional deficiencies: mild iron-deficiency anaemia is common and Rastafarians or others on strict vegetarian diets, beside their risk of rickets, may need supplements of vitamin C or folic acid to prevent more complex anaemias.
— Premature development of the breasts is statistically a little more common in Afro-Caribbean girls and is seen earlier than in other ethnic groups. It may occur as early as four or five years but is not accompanied by other signs of puberty or of any disease. There is no need for either anxiety or specialist investigation but this may not be known in many white populations where small numbers of black young girls are seen by family doctors. Similarly, these girls sometimes show equally harmless early development of pubic hair.

The risks of travel

Of course modern travellers, whatever their nationality, are at risk of acquiring or transmitting tropical diseases unfamiliar to the UK. The aim should be that universal standards of health care, immunology and treatment are available for all to standards specified by the World Health Organisation.

Psychiatric illness among British Afro-Caribbeans

Littlewood and Lipsedge (1988) comment that in general immigrants tend to have a higher rate of mental illness than the people among whom they settle and they are not surprised that this should be so for British West Indians but they are concerned and puzzled that the diagnosis rate for 'schizophrenia' is between three and five times that for the white population (e.g. Rwegellera 1977, Littlewood and Lipsedge 1981).

Clare (1994) is concerned, with reason, that the diagnostic term schizophrenia, although defined with increasing precision within the American and International Classifications of Disease (American Psychiatric Association 1987, World Health Organisation 1988), is becoming useless or harmful because it is so devalued and misunderstood in politics and in debate within the media. By analogy with the lessening of stigma and better quality of debate attached to the disappearance of labels such as 'mongol', a condition now referred to as Down's Syndrome after the physician who identified it, and Alzheimer's Disease rather than pre-senile dementia, Clare says that we should stop using the word schizophrenia and attach some new name, such as Bleuler's Disease, after the psychiatrists (father and son) who first described the condition, in the hope that the ensuing debate will generate more light and less heat. However, the research to which this chapter briefly refers, and to which of course we do not do justice with regard to the complexity of the issues involved, is based on well-defined and agreed use of the International Classification of Diseases. It is not just a matter of politics and journalism but requires continued work.

The theories offered include:

— people at risk of psychiatric illness may be more likely to migrate;
— the experience itself is stressful and increases the risk of illness;
— the struggle within a framework of limited opportunity is very stressful;
— there may be cultural variations in how immigrants respond to

adversity;
— there may be problems about using services provided until an
  emergency occurs;
— birth events and childhood infections may be relevant.

It is also thought (as discussed in the above references) that European psychiatrists may not be good at diagnosing psychotic illnesses
in people from differing cultures. It may be that short-lived
responses to stress are misdiagnosed as schizophrenia (Littlewood
and Lipsedge 1981, Littlewood and Cross 1980, McGovern and Cope
1987, Littlewood 1986). In a BMA editorial (1988) Littlewood and
Lipsedge write: 'It appears that depressed West Indians seldom seek
psychiatric treatment, are seldom offered admission, and if they are
admitted they are likely to be diagnosed as schizophrenics. Suicide
among Afro-Caribbeans is less common than among whites, while
overdoses are equally common in those over age twenty-five but
lower among those under twenty-five. Whether Caribbeans actually
do have lower rates of minor psychiatric problems (which seems
unlikely), the psychiatric perception of their illnesses is that they are
more somatic' (i.e. expressed in terms of bodily symptoms): 'West
Indians are seldom offered psychotherapy and are more likely to be
given electro-convulsive therapy and higher doses of medication.'

They report also that there was an over-representation of black
patients in secure units and special hospitals (McGovern and Cope
1987, Littlewood 1986).

They record that there has been found no strong evidence for the
possibility that West Indians were more reluctant to admit to psychiatric illness or that they were more likely to behave aggressively
before being admitted to hospital. The black community in the UK
has continued to argue that these figures are related to racism in psychiatry (Francis 1994).

Sashidharan and Francis (1993) take an overview of research
which relates ethnicity to mental illness. In their view, only one
study (Harrison *et al.* 1988) establishes the basis for the long task of
studying the relative incidence of schizophrenia in black and white
populations, yet this was a study of samples of identified patients.
Incidence in general population samples is yet to be established.

The problems of defining black and white and of controlling for
patterns of immigration, socio-economic factors and other factors
currently researched in the general field of epidemiology mean that
there is still a long road to travel when attempting to compare the
incidence of major mental illness in those from varying ethnic or
racial groups.

Ahmad (1993) editor of *'Race' and Health in Contemporary Britain*,
to which Sashidharan and Francis contribute, comments that study

of the Irish population in Britain shows that, a century after substantial migration from the nineteenth century famine in Ireland, there are still visible differences in health and prosperity between the Irish and the host population. Disadvantage may not link only with skin colour and is slow to fade.

Black women are over-represented in the current prison system, representing 23 per cent of that population yet only 5 per cent of the general population in the UK. The Howard League (1993), which provides this figure, is of the view that this over-representation is because black women do not conform with stereotyped expectations of the white judges and magistrates who sentence them. In their view, women in general do not merit custodial sentences, being inappropriately imprisoned for offences better dealt with in other ways. They are concerned that medical and probation reports often contain superfluous information on the mothering capacities of women and that these are taken into account when sentences are formulated. They quote the current cost to the tax payer of imprisonment as being £563 per week per woman and consider that this money would be better spent on improved childcare and probation facilities.

The future pattern

It has been hoped that, as with the children who did less well in school immediately after immigration, the establishment of reliable patterns of childcare and family life will be followed by better school achievement and mental health for younger and next generation immigrants. Disturbingly, it is recorded that the children of West Indian immigrants continue to show higher admission rates for psychotic illnesses. Littlewood and Lipsedge (1988) write that they think that this continued increase may be linked to 'a precipitation of schizophrenia in those vulnerable by the experience of racism refracted through subtle cognitive changes, including selfhood, autonomy and locus of control'. They propose long-term studies both of the young population, mainly under age thirty when studied, who were showing these worryingly high rates of psychiatric illness, so that it could be discovered whether they recovered over time and that the few cases of illness in the older population should also be evaluated. As West Indians become valued equal members of our society, patterns of illness may not differ from those in the indigenous population, an aim which may be slow to achieve, requiring greater social change than has yet been envisaged.

Indeed it may not happen at all: the improved physical health and education prospects for the young, which have shown up during the last two decades, are in process of erosion by repeated re-organisation which risks the fragmentation of health, education and social services while eroding links between them (Bennathan 1992); yet improved mental health services for the whole population, together with better treatment by the criminal justice system, would be of benefit both to the former immigrant and to the indigenous populations of the UK as we move into the next century.

Bhopal and White (1993) establish the main types of research for the promotion of good health in ethnic minority groups as follows:

1. Studies of the impact of social policy and social circumstances on the health of ethnic minorities.

2. Epidemiological studies of the health status, including risk factors and the determinants of health, of ethnic minority groups.

3. Research to establish the appropriate principles and information base to guide the development and evaluation of health promotion interventions for ethnic minorities.

These principles for practice, to look at populations, social policies, socio-economic circumstances and risk factors alert researchers that ethnicity is difficult to measure since populations are varied, research aims are not always clear and because ethnocentricity of the researchers may affect both the interpretation and the use of the data obtained (Senior and Bhopal 1993). These are themes to which we turn in our next chapter.

The children's stories

Tales of what goes wrong are more readily available in health education and family law records than are tales of success. The following, complied from many case records, are characteristic of the ill-fated combination of immigrant children and their families with limited health and social care resources, both in the Caribbean and in the UK.

Amalie (born 1950) and Vincent (born 1966)

Amalie came to the UK from the parish of St Elizabeth in Jamaica at the age of twelve. She had lived until then with her grandmother. She joined her mother, mother's boyfriend and two small children in a high-rise flat in Hackney. A.L. Hendriks (1965) describes her heritage:

Road to Lacovia

This is a long, forbidding road, a narrow,
hard aisle of asphalt under
a high gothic arch of bamboos.
Along it a woman drags a makeshift barrow
in slanting rain, and thunder:
a thin woman who wears no shoes.

This is St Elizabeth, a hard parish
to work; but when you are born
on land, you want to work that land.
Nightfall comes here swift and harsh and deep, but garish
flames of lightning show up torn
cheap clothing barely patched, and

a face patterned by living. Every sharp line
of this etching has the mark
of struggle. To the eye, unyielding
bleak earth has brought her close to famine;
yet through this wild descent of dark
this woman dares to walk, and sing.

By 1966 Amalie was pregnant. She moved in with her boyfriend and gave birth to Vincent.

For the next five years Amalie moved between her boyfriend, her mother's flat and a series of bedsits. Vincent was 'received into care' as an emergency on nine different occasions between 1967 and 1969. Each time his mother would leave him only for two or three weeks and then reclaimed him; the longest he was away was six weeks.

In 1971 when Vincent was five years old, he was to be seen in a small children's home. Indeed, it was not possible to miss Vincent. He ran between one room and another, never still, his activity seemed without purpose and he did not play. If anyone spoke to him he did not look them in the eye yet at times he would rush to cuddle and be held. Sometimes he would have a violent temper tantrum. He ate voraciously even though his weight and height were appropriate to his age and there was no history he had ever been ill-nourished. He was in good general health and physically forward for his age, though it was difficult to assess his vocabulary since he spoke very little. His social worker said that there were no grounds to take care proceedings concerning Vincent. His mother cared for him well and if she did get into difficulties would always ask for help. She was planning to take him home again as soon as she had 'sorted herself out'.

In 1978, aged twelve, Vincent was living full-time in a children's home run by a national charity. This was in a pleasant small market town about thirty miles from London. Legally his mother was still his guardian and no care proceedings had ever been taken, but by the time Vincent was eight his mother had said that she could not look after him full-time. Vincent was getting into a lot of difficulty at school. His reading was still only at a five year old level and he continued to throw lots of temper tantrums, by now this happened in class so that he was very difficult to manage along with the other children. He was big for his age and well-nourished and when he did not get his own way during play would hit or kick at his classmates.

In those days there were residential boarding schools maintained and paid for by the Inner London Education Authority and Vincent was offered a place when nine years old. The plan was that he would spend Mondays to Fridays each week in the school, where small classes and intensive supervision would help him both with his basic educational skills and with his ability to get along with other children and teachers. Weekends and school holidays would be spent in the care of his mother who by now had a new partner and a two year old baby. During the next three years Vincent had continued at the school but his visits home had become less frequent and shorter and 'respite care' had been offered during a number of school holidays by the children's charity.

Then, when Vincent was thirteen years old, he was excluded from his special school after he had broken another child's arm during a fight in the playground. He had missed his last two home visits and by default was now living full-time in the children's home. In 1981 Vincent was referred to a child psychiatric service for a report by a Juvenile Court. He had been found guilty of breaking and entering into a number of shops and was in breach of a probation order. By the age of sixteen years he was in local authority secure accommodation. He lived briefly with his mother after his release and then embarked on his first prison sentence.

At twenty, Vincent was a father but he and his seventeen year old partner broke up after he had struck her during the pregnancy. His partner Charlene had been born in the UK, in 1967, to a couple from Barbados who had settled in Birmingham. They were angry and upset that Charlene had got pregnant so young but she moved back with her family and her baby Erroll began to grow up, as he might have done in Barbados, in a three generation family. When he was last heard of he was doing well in primary school. Vincent's whereabouts are unknown to his family.

Marsha (born 1962)

Like Amalie, Marsha grew up with her grandmother in Jamaica and came to England at the age of thirteen years. She tells how she and her younger brother got on a plane at Kingston airport and did not know where they were going. Marsha now thinks that her grandmother, who was in poor health, could not bear to tell them that they were going to England for good, and her account was very vague, that Marsha and the little one would go for a holiday. Today Marsha recalls how she wept all the way on the plane and how, when she got to Heathrow Airport, she did not recognise the mother whom she had last seen eight years earlier. Her little brother had been only two when his mother had left for England.

The two children, like Amalie, moved into mother's new flat. For the first time they met their stepfather and three children under the age of six years. Marsha's memory is that the little ones were well cared for and loved but that she in particular was expected to be housemaid and cleaner for the family, particularly when her mother was at work.

Marsha says that she ran away from home after being beaten by her stepfather with a belt. He would tell the children that that was how he had been brought up.

Marsha was fostered with an English family, and though she had struggled to learn 'standard' English during her two years at a local school, she still found it very hard to communicate. At sixteen she moved out to live with Greg, a boy whose history was very similar to her own and who had moved from his English home with the father whom he had known only from the age of fourteen years.

Marsha and Greg are still together in the 1990s. Their tragedy is that their firstborn child died of a brain haemorrhage after being violently shaken, aged four months. This was in 1980. The next baby was taken into care at eight months old. There had been very strict supervision by the local authority since there was obviously justified anxiety as to whether the young couple would cope better with their second baby and, when a twist fracture of the arm was diagnosed such that the paediatricians were certain this could not have happened accidentally, the second child was placed for adoption.

Today Marsha can speak very vividly of her loneliness, grief and anger after the death of the first child, the guilt which she felt and her longing to be looked after herself by a loving family now that she was a mother.

Greg and Marsha stayed together and were lucky in finding deep and satisfying support from the London-based Pentecostal church, very similar to those which their grandmothers had attended. Eight years after the death of their firstborn, Greg and Marsha again became parents and are successfully bringing up two children who are now in primary school.

Wynona

Wynona, aged fifteen, came to the attention of health services at a point when she was smashing up the furniture in a local authority children's home and threatening to 'beat on' anybody who tried to stop her. Wynona's story was rather like that of Marsha, she had joined her English mother and younger siblings at the age of twelve. She had entered her local school at least three years behind in reading and number work and in class would sit gazing into space and looking as though she didn't understand.

Between twelve and fourteen years Wynona put on a lot of weight and by now was five foot six inches tall and weighed twelve stone. She got excluded from school after being in a fight with two white girls who, though the same age, were of much slighter build and then Wynona's mother refused to have the girl at home, saying that she too was scared of her.

At the point when the small children's home contained staff who were also scared of Wynona and not sure what to do next, the medical officer called in to 'help', tried to admit the girl to a psychiatric ward.

She was very indignant that no beds were available; the norm being that child and adolescent psychiatric units were small and provided only a few beds per thousand population compared with the resources available for adults. Moreover, the psychiatric unit said, having sent a doctor on a domiciliary visit, that Wynona was not 'mentally ill' but was showing the kind of temper tantrums that were understandable if one thought of her as acting several years younger than her calendar age. Their advice, and they offered support on this, was that Wynona and anyone looking after her needed help in controlling, containing and setting limits to the child's bad behaviour and also providing goals and rewards for behaving suitably. This seemed impossible to the children's home staff and indeed to Wynona's mother who in effect were rewarding Wynona with a great deal of attention, shock and horror whenever the girl had another 'outburst'. To make matters worse, the care staff and Wynona's mother talked of the child's behaviour as 'fits', implying that all of this was beyond their or Wynona's control.

Wynona was indeed admitted briefly to a children's ward and quite heavily sedated as a way of calming everyone's anxiety. She eventually did much better when found a place in a small specialist day school and was able to return to the care of her mother. (Resources such as this have shrunk in number during the last decade and this solution might not be available today.) Moreover, Wynona managed to avoid being labelled as psychiatrically ill, thus avoiding adding to the statistics concerning mental illness in West

Indian immigrants.

None of these stories is characteristic specifically of West Indians. Dislocation, overwhelmed parents, social isolation, financial and housing problems, under-stimulation of children and limited opportunities for learning social skills can all happen within indigenous populations and in any immigrant group.

However, for twenty years, particularly in inner cities, West Indian children and parents were particularly visible and their difficulties such as to make quite dramatic impact on health services, courts and social workers. And there were disadvantages in the Caribbean countries from which these immigrants had journeyed. The rich threads of their cultural heritage were fragmented by colonialism and slavery, the deteriorating home economy of the 1970s had created a framework in which those who longed for their roots could not go back. Family networks had been broken asunder. The 'mother country' wanted reliable, inexpensive labour rather than new generations. It is perhaps a matter for pride and rejoicing that so many successes balance tragedy and failure.

And today, for some, return does occur. A couple, now sixty, who left May Pen, Jamaica thirty-five years ago have now bought a bungalow there and plan to live with their daughter and grandchildren on pensions from the National Health Service and British Rail. Their grandchildren will go to the local primary school, sing in the choir of a family church and go on to further education. For some, a long road has led home again, albeit to an island itself engrossed in rapid social change. There is no going back to the past.

6 Ethnicity, race and racism

Case-History, Jamaica

In 19-something X was born
in Jubilee Hospital, howling, black.

In 19- (any date plus four)
X went to school.
They showed him pretty pictures
of his Queen.

When he was 7, in elementary school,
he asked what naygas were.
In secondary school he knew.
He asked in History one day
where slaves came from.
'Oh, Africa,' the master said,
'Get on with your work.'

Up at the university he didn't find himself;
and, months before he finally dropped out,
would ramble round the campus late at night
and daub his blackness on the walls.

(Mervyn Morris 1973)

Introduction

The word 'race' is so varied and flexible in its meaning as to be virtually useless in work with people from ethnic minority groups or in formulating the law. The word 'racist' is perhaps more useful. It has come to mean using ideas or perceptions about race in a pejorative way so that the *racist negatively discriminates* against members of other ethnic groups. Rather than classifying people, it is more realistic to legislate against racism and to define the civil rights of individual members of different racial groups: the aim should be to provide laws equally available to all citizens and anti-racist laws which protect minorities. It is a pity that the word 'ethnic' has become devalued in common use, often being used as an alternative to 'black', a term equally obscure and unclear. In practice the terms 'racial' and 'ethnic' are used to cover a variety of concepts.

Most European countries have populations derived from a range of sources over time. Britain alone contains human beings, until recently all more or less the same skin colour, ranging from blonde, blue-eyed Nordic people, probably the descendants of Viking invaders, via dark Gaelic-speaking Celts to descendants of the Angles, Saxons and Jutes who, we were all taught, were the Ancient Britons before the Romans came, adding in turn their quota of genes from around the Mediterranean. Then came the Normans, themselves a mongrel race. Britain has long been a maritime nation and traders from all parts of the world have landed on our shores: some of them have stayed. For at least nine centuries Jewish traders, intellectuals and refugees have entered the islands. The Hugenots were refugees in the eighteenth century and, until the urbanisation of Britain hindered them, travelling people from across Europe have included Britain in their wanderings.

In turn, either of necessity, as during the Highland clearances of the eighteenth century, or from forced choice as when younger sons of landed gentry were sent out to the colonies, or as merchant sailors and in the armed forces, Britons have travelled the world and settled wherever they roamed.

Only during the last forty years however have large numbers of people settled here who are of obviously and immediately different appearance. The words 'ethnic minority' which equally could have applied to Romans, Normans, Jews from Eastern Europe or Hugenots, have come to be applied in the main to people of a different skin colour. But the term 'ethnic minority member' should be applicable in any country to an individual who, not only by reason of skin colour but because of other physical characteristics, religion, language or cultural differences could be distinguished from the majority. Such a person might have lived here for one, two or many generations. Thus, the term should have been applicable to George III and his household or to travelling people, Poles, Hungarians, Jews of many nationalities, Catholics in Northern Ireland, Welsh or Gaelic speakers, Asian Africans, Indian or Pakistani Muslims or Hindus, Africans of many backgrounds and, from the Caribbean, people of many cultures, skin colours, religions and languages.

The British House of Windsor dates from 1915; its former name was Saxe-Coburg-Gotha and its origin within the complex network of European and Russian states which existed before World War I. For children born to the partnership between members of different cultures, religions or nationalities the result is complex, as within the British Royal Family whose cousins were German, Austrian and Russian.

Zeitlin *et al.* (1990) studied concepts of race and ethnicity on behalf of the Child and Adolescent Psychiatry Specialist Section of the Royal College of Psychiatrists. This chapter draws on that work.

The Oxford English Dictionary describes the word 'ethnic' as being an adjective: 'Pertaining to race, ethnological (whence the noun ethnicity); gentile, heathen; of a special racial, linguistic etc. group (usually a minority)'. The Greek root *ethnikos* is given as meaning 'heathen' and *ethnos* as 'nation'.

Race

Race is defined as:

1. Group of persons or animals or plants connected by common descent, posterity of person; house, family, tribe or nation regarded as of common stock; distinct ethnical stock; genus or species or breed or variety of animals or plants, any great division of living creatures (the human, feathered, four-footed etc., race).
2. Descent, kindred, (of noble, Oriental etc., race; separate in language and race).
3. Class of persons etc. with some common feature (the race of poets, dandies etc.).
4. (race) relations (between members of different races in same country).

Discriminating

This is an adjective defined as 'discerning, acute'. To discriminate well is a skill. To discriminate (a verb) is 'to single out a particular person or group for special favour or disfavour, to recognise or understand differences, to constitute or mark a difference, to be discerning in matters of taste'. Although to be discriminating is a quality or gift the process of discrimination is described (Collins Dictionary) as '1. Unfair treatment of a person, racial group or minority etc.; action based on prejudice'. Second and third meanings are 'subtle appreciation of matters of taste' and 'the ability to see fine distinctions and differences'.

It is a pity that this valuable word, indicating the possession of fine skills in distinction and observation, has come, as a noun, to imply negative qualities. This is a recent event related to the process of discrimination as a way of singling out, as inadequate, inferior or worthy of second rate treatment, members of particular groups, usually because of skin colour, but often also because of their sex or age. It would be better if the words 'negative discrimination' were kept together to remind us that the process of discrimination in itself is at worst neutral or at best a positive one. In common usage however the word 'discriminate' has become to 'discriminate against' or to treat as second best.

Inheritance

Skin colour, physiognomy and other physical characteristics are inherited. These include facial characteristics, eye colour, average weight and height and, more controversially since this is so hard to measure, there may be differences between racial groups in cognition or in common linguistic, artistic and athletic skills, just as there are genetic differences between members of families.

It is not a simple matter to identify membership of a racial group for the purpose of comparison. In sport, for example, the simplistic precept 'black Americans are the best sprinters' at the 1960 Olympics was not borne out by the results, despite selective training and entry yet such precepts may cause children to be selected as likely to possess specific attributes while other potential qualities remain unexplored or undervalued. For example, American coaches direct young black athletes towards basketball or running. It is important, as research is attempted, that old myths are not ratified nor new ones created, and that recognition is given to the proposition that differences 'within' ethnic groups may be as great as, or greater than, those 'between' groups.

There is less controversy in recognising that some racial groups are genetically at risk of particular disorders; the commonest and the best researched for the Caribbean is the incidence of sickle cell anaemia. On such issues as this, doctrinaire refusal to monitor genetically linked illness among ethnic minority groups has given way to the commonsense application of routine health care screening as described in Chapter 5.

Culture

This is a complicated concept and previous chapters have indicated the richness and variety available within a set of islands.

> Are we not blended and caught from old
> pigments? What new crucible heats
> and fuses our proud mixture? Where
> are our colours burnt? In what bright mould?

> Have we not taken ebonys and crimsons,
> Ochres and pale ecrus of loves
> deeper than blood for the making of
> our harmonies? We the tawny ones.

> (A. L. Hendriks 1988)

Culture refers (in dictionary terms) to 'Improvement or refinement by education and training'. The personal experience of children is to be distinguished from those associations linked with their family of birth and place of origin. A child's personal experiences are more relevant to the development of skills for coping with life's vicissitudes and a sense of oneself in time and place. Children do better in this search or, at least, may find it easier, if they grow up with a minimum of uncertainty and instability and if the family with whom they live is well-defined and their relationship with that family is clear cut.

It is a mistake to impose on a child stereotyped, over-simplified or rigid 'cultural identity'. The same applies to religion. There is a difference between encouraging a child to study, for example, the Hindu or Presbyterian religion of his forebears and insisting that he must practise it wherever he lives and whatever his own education, or that Asian English adolescents must not wear sports clothing irrespective of their own wishes, or that dietary restrictions or refusal of medical treatment should put a child at risk. If a child is to acquire a place in a complex and changing world the need is for a sense of history and the richness of origins, not that the child be fitted into a pre-ordained and rigid mould. Education should enrich, not constrain.

Identity

This concept, yet again a complex one, may be considered in terms of assigned and personal identity. That which is assigned is determined by social circumstances including sex, place and country of residence, social class, income, religion, ethnic origins and a host of other variables which may be accepted, fought against or reluctantly complied with. Personal identity inevitably is linked with these specific situational and historical factors but also is a characteristic of the unique individual.

Laungani (1994), in considering the effects of bereavement in Asian and English families, speaks of a continuum between concepts of individualism and communalism such that the salient attitudes, behaviours and values of people may be represented at any point along it and may change over time in either direction. Western families, in his view, are to the left of the spectrum, valuing conditions which do not permit easy sharing of problems and worries, respecting individual 'physical and psychological space' with strict unspoken rules about touching and encroachment. He contrasts that with communities where an extended family network, the use of the collective pronoun 'we' rather than 'I' and suppression of personal identity within the collective identity of family and community, are valued as in traditional Asian communities. Conflict between a search for an individual identity and sustenance of, or submission to, a family or group identity, presents problems to immigrants, particularly to those whose appearance and heritage differ markedly from those of the host population.

Self-esteem

There are problems with the term 'self-esteem' which also is used as though it had a commonly agreed, uncontroversial meaning. This is not so. Triseliotis (1983a) writes: 'Personal identity is the result of multiple psychological, social and cultural influences which combine towards the building of an integrated and unified self. By personal identity I mean the kind of consciousness we all carry about – "who" we are and the kind of self-image we have of ourselves. Depending on its quality and strength, the sense of self gives us a feeling of separateness from others, distinguishing us from our environment, whilst at the same time enabling us to enter into daily social interaction and relationships with a degree of confidence.'

Triseliotis' study at the Department of Social Work Education, University of Edinburgh identified three factors which make a substantial contribution to identity formation:

— the childhood experience of feeling wanted and loved within a secure environment;
— knowledge about one's background and personal history; and
— the experience of being perceived by others as a worthwhile person.

Each of these factors complements the others: Triseliotis' research makes it clear that factors two and three can be attained when factor one has been made available to the child. For example, among children adopted and fostered, those best able to search for and understand their origins are those who have been brought up to feel secure, wanted and worthwhile.

In this context, assigned identity can be either a privilege or a burden. To be labelled, for example, as 'black' may provide access to a rich range of cultural information. It may be a form of negative discrimination, assigning the black person to supposed membership of a second rate, incompetent or criminal group or it may be, for example throughout the whole of Africa, the majority experience.

The child of mixed race

To be assigned to the categorisation 'black' when a child is of mixed parentage is contentious and less than helpful.

Tizard and Phoenix (1989, 1993) discuss the trend, in the 1980s, for labelling all children of mixed race as black and for placing children so labelled within 'black' families. They summarise the arguments then put forward to justify this practice as follows: 'It is said that black children living in white families fail to develop a "positive black identity". Instead they suffer identity confusion and development of self concept, believing or wishing that they were white.'

It is further argued that, unless very carefully trained, families with white skins cannot help black children to achieve coping skills and survival techniques needed for dealing with racist practice in society at large.

Thirdly it is argued that children placed in white families will grow up unable to relate to black people and yet will be rejected by those with white skins.

All these arguments are contentious and should become the subject of informed debate and research rather than polemic. Those who support them cite clinical and personal stories, often told with great passion. It was recognised, when looking at some of the early studies on black children in white families (e.g. Gill and Jackson 1983) that in the early days of transracial adoption most such children did indeed grow up, along with the families to which they had been transplanted, in predominantly white, middle-class areas. They were said to be at risk of losing their identity and of being vulnerable to discrimination in adolescence and adult life.

Gill and Jackson found that the children were doing very well by a whole range of criteria and were more sophisticated than had been supposed, being able to describe themselves as of mixed race or brown rather than black and, in particular, distinguishing between being of Asian or Afro-Caribbean origin. They could discuss the ways in which they were different from Asian and West Indian children and it was clear they did not feel close to these groups but that sense of self and self-esteem were high. Moreover, they were not unable to relate to black people nor did they despise themselves because they were a different skin colour from the majority around them. However, Gill and Jackson qualified their findings, pointing out that the children studied were still young. Black (1991) and Lau (1993) overview earlier research and preconceptions and discuss principles for practice.

Tizard and Phoenix point out that the discussion about self-esteem and identity among teenagers of different skin colour from the majority lacks comparison groups of those who have grown up either in their own families or in 'matched families'. Helping children to do well is far more complex than matching (and imprecisely at that) the skin colour of caretakers and children.

A review of the research on self-perception of young black children living with their own parents indicates substantial reliance on a technique developed by two black psychologists, Clark and Clark (1947), in the USA. They presented small children between three and seven years with black (then called Negro) and white dolls which looked exactly the same except for their skin and hair colour. Those early studies indicated that the children could correctly identify the black and white dolls but when asked 'Give me the nice doll' would choose one with a white skin and also a third of them, when asked 'Give me the doll that looks like you', also chose the white doll and half identified a black doll with 'the doll that looks bad'. White children in contrast preferred the white doll, selected the black doll as bad and knew that the white one looked like them.

Many other researchers found similar results. It was thought that this meant that the black children rejected themselves and had low self-esteem, taking on board the way white people viewed their skin colour. Indeed, this research influenced the 1950s desegregation of schools in the USA.

By the 1970s the studies were more sophisticated, using dolls which resembled children in features as well as in skin colour and also using photographs and adding the possibility that children could identify themselves as of mixed race. However, Davey and Norburn (1980) found that only between one and two thirds of the children, ranging in age from seven to ten years, chose a photograph of a child in their own racial group as the one 'they would most like to be'. This was similar in Asian and West Indian children whereas white children of the same age almost always chose a photograph of a child with the same skin colour as themselves. (These children probably understood their society better than the researchers.)

In another study (Bagley and Coard 1975, further discussed in

Bagley and Young 1979), only 57 per cent of a sample of West Indian children aged five to ten years said they did *not* want to change their skin colour whereas 88 per cent of white children were happy the way they were. There have been few studies of adolescents but in Jamaica in the 1960s high school children preferred European features, straight hair and straight noses. Those who approximated more closely to 'European' features and hair were considered most attractive. (Jamaicans colloquially would speak of 'good noses' and 'bad noses', 'good hair' and 'bad hair'.) This is not surprising, given that they would learn 'You white, all right, You brown, stick aroun', You black, stand back' – an ironic nursery rhyme fashioned by adults. Today Jamaican television advertising glamourises 'brownings' – mixed race men and women with light skin – no wonder children show that they recognise this.

Wilson (1987) in a more sophisticated study of colour preferences, in children of black, white and mixed race, found a 'hopeful' overall picture, that children from minority groups 'were a long way from the archetype of the tortured personality split between two conflicting cultures'. Mixed race children could 'be themselves'. She considered that a facilitating environment was critical to their wellbeing and recommended continuing research, a point emphasised by Tizard and Phoenix in the work discussed below.

However, there are also studies to show that identifying with a racial minority and being concerned about this, and being aware that one's race is regarded with prejudice, does not necessarily mean that a child has low self-esteem. Personal identity, whatever the racial group, is linked with the factors identified by Triseliotis and first depends on the availability of reliable love and care.

Tizard and Phoenix (1993), taking as their starting point current controversies on whether children with black skins can be successfully reared by white adults, built on their earlier critical evaluation of research on transracial placements and concepts of identity by setting up a research project funded by the Department of Health. Their recent book, with another to follow, brings alive the experiences of 180 young people of whom one third were white, one third black, with two African or Afro-Caribbean parents and one third with parents of whom one was white and one black. They were in mainstream schooling, between the ages of fourteen and sixteen years and living in their own homes with at least one parent. Their starting point was that current opinion about the developmental needs, and the experience of racism, of black children in a white society was politicised, anecdotal or drawn from small numbers of children with specialist needs who were unable to live with their birth families and oversimplified the concept of a dichotomy of black *vis à vis* white.

They point out that in the USA there are now more than one million mixed race (black/white) children and adults. Tizard and Phoenix hypothesise that, with increased acceptance of interracial marriage and a more sophisticated approach to childrearing and education, young people are likely to be able to identify and sustain identities specific to themselves. They comment however that they had difficulty in finding their sample of 60 mixed race teenagers since, in the UK, more than half of all mixed race people are under ten years old. Of the black parents, only two were born within the UK compared with 88 per cent of their children. Of the mixed race children, few had the experience of living only with the black parent, the commonest outcome where a marriage broke up was that the mixed race children remained with a white mother.

The researchers set the scene by discussing the historical context of black settlement in this country and the concepts of scientific racism dating from the eugenics movement of the early twentieth century when racial intermarriage was discouraged because of the mistaken belief that the white stock would be weakened, or that the worst genetic traits of each race would be reproduced in the offspring. These views, agonisingly enacted during the Second World War, were not formally discredited by scientists until the 1950s and even after the Second World War thirty out of forty-eight states in the USA still retained laws against racial intermarriage. The Supreme Court ended such laws only in 1967.

The writers further point out that, in the UK, such intermarriages as did occur tended to be in ports such as Cardiff and Liverpool and London where black sailors lived in companionship with white women. The children of communities such as this were disadvantaged, not just because at that time mixed parentage was stigmatised but because of social isolation, fathers who earned their living at sea, poor educational qualifications and a colour bar which existed in many communities throughout the UK at that time. Indeed, it is likely that children from mixed marriages were then stigmatised to a greater extent than the minority of children with two black parents.

Meanwhile, within the Caribbean there were exquisitely accurate categorisations of skin colour. As slavery ended, there was a hierarchy of skin colour from white to black and the whole society was profoundly race and colour conscious. Terms now simply considered pejorative, such as 'mulatto', the child of a white man and a black woman, 'sambo', a child of a mulatto and a negro, 'quadroon', the child of a mulatto woman and a white man, 'mustee', the child of a quadroon and a white man, through to 'octoroon', child of a quadroon and a white man were used much as animal breeders might categorise sheep or horses. 'Freed mulattos' formed a separate caste, would marry each other and would attempt to lighten the skins of their children (James 1994). This careful stratification did not survive in the USA where, after emancipation, people, as in modern South Africa, were classified as black if they had any known 'negro' ancestry. Despite this, as in the Jamaican rhyme, there has been a general assumption that people with lighter skins and Caucasian features carried greater prestige. The 'black is beautiful, one drop of black blood means that you are black' philosophy which has been of such political importance and value during the last decade is the mirror image of this earlier stratification. Now, to be black is to be 'proud' and to deny one's black heritage is to 'deny one's identity'. (Why should anyone be 'proud' of the colour of their skin except as an antidote to all the denigration of dark-skinned people?)

Tizard and Phoenix began their research with the hypothesis that these extreme positions are inappropriate and over-simple for the new generations of mixed race and black children within the UK. Their work does indeed give some credence to this position, should be read in its entirety and, given its great importance, should be repeated over time. They comment that a 1989 labour force survey found that of people from the Caribbean who were marrying or living together, 27 per cent of men and 28 per cent of women had white partners; the likelihood that children of mixed race will be able to find friends similar to themselves, a problem for some in the current sample, will decrease over time.

Asked whether they thought of themselves as black, only 39 per cent of the mixed race children said this, the rest said no, and in a sophisticated fashion, discussed their various allegiances. Many indeed were capable of complex discussions about their racial heritage and identity and many resisted colour labels. They were prepared to use a number of terms such as 'brown', 'mixed race' and even 'half-caste' (a term which the older generation had thought pejorative) when speaking of themselves and of others like them.

They were able to speak of their attachment to a white parent, more often in this sample the mother, and to state with great clarity that they did not wish, by speaking of themselves as 'black', to diminish or deny some of the most important attachments in their lives.

Some of those going to multi-racial schools had found that other children did not think of them as black and had experienced 'racist' remarks from black as well as from white children. This feeling of being different troubled some of the group yet many regarded their identity as an interesting advantage. 60 per cent felt 'proud' of their identity, seeing many advantages in it. (We have increasing reservations about the use of the word pride in situations like this but it is common currency.)

The parental sample interviewed was small but did not demonstrate that people of black skin colour were better able than those of white skin colour to educate young people about racism. They discussed, in vivid and lively terms, a range of strategies for being part of a mixed couple, for educating their children about the two sides of their heritage and for dealing with racial insults in school and in the community. Of the young people from the three groups, four out of five of the black children and half of those of mixed parentage preferred black youth music, so did a quarter of the white students. These London-based children showed considerable knowledge of black youth styles and black radio stations though few read the British Caribbean press unless this was available through adult members of the family.

Many young people resisted the idea that there are separate and distinct black and white cultures, the majority arguing that today there is a good deal of overlap. They were able to discuss their concept of themselves as British ('English' was thought of as having a white connotation whereas the term 'British' does not) or as Londoners. Of those who did not expect to live as adults in Britain the majority thought in terms of moving to the USA and Europe rather to Africa or the Caribbean.

All the young people who had encountered racism were able to describe the strategies for dealing with it; 15 per cent claimed never to have experienced racism and the authors comment that this arguably may be a first line of defence used without thinking about it rather than, as with more aware young people, in a conscious way, since many describe ignoring or walking away from racist experiences. This defusion of racist comment often is seen as an effective strategy but is not always recognised as such. Experiences of course were difficult to quantify and compare, one child might identify as racist an experience which others did not consider to be discriminatory.

There was large variation in the help available to the young people; only 57 per cent said that their parents had advised them and, whereas some multi-racial comprehensive schools had a clear-cut policy, strategies for dealing with racism were rarely an overt part of the curriculum. Opportunities to discuss, and perhaps role-play, the various strategies were lacking. The researchers found no evidence however that, where advice was given, black parents were more likely to tell the children that they should be 'proud' of their colour. (In our view this is no bad thing.) The range of differences between families concerning how to deal with racism was unrelated to colour mix or social class.

Ironically, those children who had suffered least from racism were those who were advantaged in conventional ways, coming from middle class homes. Many affluent parents with black or mixed race children had made sacrifices to send their children to independent schools, arguing that high standards of education, the acquisition of social skills and self-esteem would enable their children to cope better in any society (note the comments by educationists in Chapter 4). As much racism was reported in multi-racial schools as in white ones yet this concealed a gender difference in that boys, in any school, were more likely to be subject to racial comment and attack than were the girls.

Alan Harris, an English university lecturer, impeccably liberal, captured the working class prejudice of his post-war childhood in a Midlands city as follows:

from **Being English**

I have good cause to hate blacks. I belong here
they don't. They paint

their houses in bright colours
caterwaul at night,
congregate in offensive
blackness ...

Ride motorbikes in turbans, sell their daughters, abuse
the national health service, go on the dole.

Well,
I have time to observe these things
being English.

His friend and collaborator A.L. Hendriks, a Jamaican writer from an upper middle class background wrote of the English.

from **Their Mouths but not their Hearts**

They treat me civilly, are indeed polite.
Always choose quickly to discuss
Sunshine, bananas, rum, calypsos
And inevitably cricket,
('Once saw your cousin keeping wicket')
But wonder if their women dream at night
About the things they've heard about us.

(*Note*: Jackie Hendriks played cricket for the West Indies.)
(Harris and Hendriks 1988)

These poems echo and illuminate the interviews of Tizard and Phoenix with today's black and mixed race children.

In summary, the researchers comment that the racial composition of the family, that is whether the young people lived with at least one black parent, with a white parent or with step-parents, did not link with whether they identified themselves as black or with how positive they felt about their racial identity. Ironically, the children who lived with black parents were less likely to feel that skin colour was central to their lives than those who lived with white parents; they were also more likely to have in the main white friends and to go to schools with mainly white children. This was related almost entirely to the affluence of the black families interviewed. It is still the case in our society that comparatively small numbers of black people live professional lives in white suburbs and send their children to fee-paying schools. Their children are a minority within a minority of the privileged.

All in all, the research indicates that the issues for black and mixed race children in current society, though not rigidly hierarchical as in nineteenth century society, are far more complex either than the negative 'one drop makes you black and inferior' position of post-war USA society or the equally simplistic 'one drop of black blood makes you black and beautiful' stance of the 1980s.

These children and their parents are living in a complex, fast-changing society where the one norm seems to be that social class, income, quality of housing and school and further education opportunities all count far more, in protection against racism, than does polemic or the skin colour of parents, a finding which links with statements by interviewees in Chapter 4.

To read Tizard and Phoenix (1993) or James and Harris (1994) alerts us that although people of black skin have been exploited, enslaved, dislocated, disadvantaged and denigrated, their future, as for us all, rests in the provision of a better quality of life for all citizens.

7   The swing of the pendulum

Dictionary Black

The first thing it says is
Opposite to white.
I say to myself
Mmhmm all right
It says
Persons with dark skins
It says
Black-hearted – dismal – grim
Angry – threatening
Black looks
Black marks
Black lists
and Black books.

Deadly – sinister – wicked – hateful
All these words to make us 'grateful'?

A kidnapped Negro on a slaveship
is a blackbird ...

That gave these people enormous wealth.

(Sista Roots 1987)

Yvonne

In 1994 Yvonne approached her fourth birthday in the care of foster parents with whom she had lived since she was two months old. They were white, London-based and in the household Yvonne was the youngest, and the only foster child, in a family of four children. She had started the rising-five class in her local primary school which contained English, Turkish, Caribbean and Asian children.

Her mother, an English girl, at seventeen years had developed a severe illness which psychiatrists diagnosed as schizophrenia using the International Classification of Diseases (WHO 1988). She met Yvonne's father, a black-skinned Trinidadian, also diagnosed as schizophrenic, when the two were day patients at a South London psychiatric hospital. The two never lived together though George, Yvonne's father, did have his name put on the baby's birth certificate. He was already the father of another child by a Jamaican partner.

Yvonne started life in a mother and baby unit in the care of her mother but was transferred to a foster home after several worrying weeks in which nurses cared for and protected the baby while Yvonne's mother Sue gazed into space. On one occasion there was a narrow escape for Yvonne from being plunged by her mother into a very hot bath.

George visited the mother and baby unit twice but when he became fit for discharge, taking regular medication, he returned to his first partner and their son. Sue's mother offered to care for Sue and the baby but flatly denied that her daughter was ill in any way, constantly exhorting Sue to try harder. Sue's father said he did not want a 'coloured' baby in the house.

The London borough in which the family lived made Yvonne a ward of court and then, with the coming of the Children Act (1989), a Care Order was made. In presenting their case to the wardship court the local authority said that their plan was that Yvonne should not return to the care of her mother since this would be unsafe and that they had explored all possibilities of placement in both the father's and mother's families, meeting a dead end.

Sue did not oppose this though she did say that when Yvonne, now two years old, was placed for adoption she would like to be able to go on visiting. She also said that Yvonne's father was Catholic and would want his daughter in a Catholic family.

What has happened since is that Yvonne has stayed in good quality substitute care until she has put down roots, become strongly attached to her older foster brother and sisters and calls her foster parents Mum and Dad. Sue is much less ill than when Yvonne was born and, like George, takes regular medication. She visits Yvonne every week and the little girl enjoys playing with 'Mummy Sue', but Sue's condition does vary. She lives partly with her mother and partly in a one-bedroom council flat but, even with regular visits from a psychiatric nurse and time in her local day hospital, Sue often neglects herself, eating erratically. Mostly she denies that she hears voices but from time to time will speak, in a matter of fact way, of her 'bad-self voice'. This voice tells her that she is dangerous and evil. She has said that Yvonne knows about this voice and can read her mother's mind.

Sue's variable state, self-neglect and sometimes acute symptoms, which involve her child, combine to create a continuous picture of a young woman not able safely to care for Yvonne. Indeed Sue has said that Yvonne must not live with her because she can look into her mother's eyes and read her mind, an alarming indication of possible risk to a child caught up in her mother's delusional system. Sue how-ever has continued to say that she would like to see her daughter as she grows up. Yvonne has remained in temporary, insecure care because the policy of the local authority is that an adoptive home for a mixed race child 'must contain one black and one white parent'. The local authority did not start the search for such a home until Yvonne was one year old because for a long time there was hope, ini-tially sustained by Sue's psychiatrist, that Yvonne's mother might recover sufficiently to take on the care of her baby. However, three years have passed since the search began and it remains unsuccess-ful.

Both Sue and the foster family have protested about this long delay.

Ronald aged two years

Ronald's story is similar to that of Yvonne in that he too is born of a single white mother. His father is from St Lucia and one grandpar-ent was Asian, the other of African origin. His whereabouts are unknown though his former partner thinks that Ronald's father returned to the Caribbean after losing his job due to cutbacks in the car industry.

She thinks that he never knew that she was pregnant with Ronald. Angela, Ronald's mother, stayed with her parents together with the baby. This went very badly because family life continued to be just as troubled as had been the case before Ronald's birth. Angela's father drank heavily and often beat her mother. Angela too was struck on many occasions.

Ronald was taken into care and fostered after he had been struck out of his mother's arms by his grandfather one Saturday night after there had been a bout of heavy drinking. Angela left home and, by the time Ronald was two, was again pregnant with a new partner. By the time the second baby was due the father, a white-skinned long distance lorry driver, had been arrested and lost his licence because of drink driving. Angela had been arrested twice for shop-lifting.

Whereas Yvonne's foster family had grown-up children and wanted to give up their role as foster parents, Ronald settled with a couple who wished to keep him. They applied to the local authority to be considered as adoptive parents but were turned down on the grounds that they were not ethnically suitable for the little boy, both being white-skinned, without other children and living in a white, middle-class area of a provincial town.

The local authority's other objection was that the foster parents lived within a few minutes' walk of the birth grandmother. She had by now separated from her heavy-drinking husband and her view was that the little boy should stay where he was but that she hoped that she as a grandmother would be allowed to visit. The foster family said that they could cope with this now that they knew they wouldn't have to get involved with Ronald's grandfather.

The foster parents obtained independent legal advice, instructed a solicitor and applied, without the support of the local authority, to adopt Ronald. Angela and Ronald's grandmother made witness statements in support of this plan.

Errol – three months to two years

Errol lost his mother when she was stabbed to death by his father. He was three months old when this happened and was found in a cot beside his mother's bleeding body. His father, a Jamaican, pleaded guilty to manslaughter, stating that he had stabbed his wife because she had provoked him, getting out of line and putting him down and taunting him. There was no evidence, other than the killer's state-ment, that Errol's mother had done anything at all which would pro-voke his anger and still less that such alleged provocation merited stabbing. But, as is common in cases of domestic violence, the plea of guilty to manslaughter was accepted, thus saving the state an expensive trial though causing great additional grief to the victim's family who in court heard her belittled and blamed for her own death (Harris Hendriks et al. 1993).

It was recommended that Errol's father, whose immigration papers were not in order, be deported once he had served his sen-tence. The only offer of a home for Errol came from his father's sister who lived in New York and who proposed to care for the baby until such time as her brother was released from prison when he also could join her household. This was not considered a realistic plan, particularly since Errol's father had a history of assaults and had twice been imprisoned before the fatal stabbing. Errol was fostered temporarily with a white family. A home was found for him eighteen months after the killing with a 56 year old aunt of his father, a Jamaican lady with a grown-up family who lived two hundred miles from Errol's former home. Errol's guardian ad litem (a social worker acting on his behalf in the civil court hearing to plan his future) was uneasy about this plan because of the aunt's age, the distance between Errol and any other relative and because he was of an age, at eighteen months, to be deeply disturbed by such a move yet too young to comprehend it. The local authority considered that the racial match outweighed any disadvantage.

A residence order was made so that Errol could live with his aunt. The local authority in the new area agreed to visit once a month.

There is no framework other than appeal whereby a court, by review or through advice from a guardian ad litem, may consider whether this decision has been adequate to the needs of so young a child, and monthly visits do not offer much opportunity for social workers to notice if things are going wrong.

Jonathan

Jonathan, aged eighteen months, was the subject of a disputed adoption. He was born to a white father, who had denied paternity, and a Trinidadian mother who became severely depressed after the birth and committed suicide. Jonathan was placed with short-term foster parents whose skin was white. This was followed by a strike of local authority social workers and then by a period when staffing was so short that the work of planning a permanent home for the baby, it being intended that he would have one black and one white parent, did not begin until towards the end of his first year. By then he was, like Yvonne, well settled in what had meant to be his temporary home and his foster parents, closely attached to him, now argued that he would do better to remain with them. They sought independent legal advice and applied to adopt Jonathan. Meanwhile the local authority, who disagreed with this plan, enquired via the international social services as to whether Jonathan's maternal grandmother, in Trinidad, could consider taking on the baby.

It is understandable that those planning the future of small children are conscious not just of their heritage and skin colour but of the potential effects upon them of racist attitudes (even though sometimes well-meant decisions or attempted decisions may hinder much more basic needs for secure and reliable attachments). Racism is a pervasive and intractable form of wrongdoing and its effects, immediate and long-term, should not be underestimated. There is powerful writing to this effect.

Hickling (1992) is a psychiatrist in Kingston, Jamaica. He writes: 'In January 1992 I spent a week at the Social Psychiatry Unit of the Maudsley Hospital [an internationally known research unit], in preparation for research work I am presently conducting in Jamaica. I rented a brand new Rover car when I arrived in England. On the following day I was stopped on a main road in Wandsworth by a police car and accosted by three policemen who leapt out of their vehicle. They said that they suspected me of driving a stolen car, as they had radioed to the computer registration centre in Swansea which had no record of the registration plates of the car. I quickly told them I was a visiting psychiatrist at the Maudsley Hospital and that I had rented the car on the previous day when I had arrived in the country. They demanded proof of ownership, and it was only when I showed them the [hire company] tag on the key ring of the car that they reluctantly let me go.'

This senior academic was told by friends and relatives that his experience was 'par for the course' for black people in London. He recalled his student days when, seeking lodgings with a white Canadian friend, the latter had no trouble whereas a black man was turned away. Earlier experience 'came at a time when I was trying desperately to cope with a shattered expectation that Britain was home'.

Maximé (1993) a clinical psychologist, writes of her therapeutic work with black children in white families. She describes 'Mary' aged 10 who, on being referred by her white parents, snarled at the black psychologist, abusing her for the colour of her skin. Later Mary said, 'I hate me! I am ugly! I am like them … black people … all ugly'. Therapeutic work in Maximé's view was linked with the child's perception of herself as a bad black person in a white family.

Maximé describes the use of 'story' cards with black children who, when seeing an identifiable black man in a group looking as if he is teaching or explaining something, described him as 'a man is disrupting a social evening of friends and the others phoned the police for him'. Maximé tells of a child able to say to himself, concerning his skin colour: 'I see myself as a spastic in a wheelchair … you expect people to watch at you, to laugh at you, to call you names'.

There are two issues here, the child's perspective on disablement as a source of shame (about which education is needed) and his equation of a skin colour different from the majority as a disability. Maximé writes with passion about the problems of black-skinned children in white families and is not far from implying that such problems are unavoidable, yet her principles for practice would be of value to any child of any skin colour in any society.

Her recommendations are that young black children should be

offered positive images and models of people with similar skin colours to themselves and that, for example in nurseries and schools, there should be opportunities for children to learn about people from a wide range of races and cultures involved in a variety of occupations and activities. She recommends that all carers, teachers and workers should be made aware of what and how to communicate to young children concerning race and culture. Children's questions should be answered honestly, racist incidents tackled clearly and calmly and information be available to adults and children. She commends, rightly, the literature provided by the Commission for Racial Equality (e.g. CRE 1989).

Yet the Code of Practice on Race Relations (1984) published by the CRE in response to the Race Relations Act of 1976 (England and Wales) itself falls into the trap of recommending 'avoidance of discrimination'. In context, it is substantially clear that the Code of Practice enjoins the avoidance of negative discrimination which is both morally wrong and unlawful yet in so doing devalues, for children and adults alike, the delicate original meaning of the word (see Chapter 6), nor does it debate the concept of positive discrimination, the possible need on occasion to single out an individual or a group with particular characteristics (race, age, sex, colour, handicap etc.) so as to provide them with enhanced opportunity or resources.

To return to children such as Yvonne, Ronald and Errol, it can be postulated that a form of 'positive discrimination', singling out, as the factor most relevant to their future, their racial and cultural background, has blinkered those responsible for considering the groundwork of knowledge common to all children about their needs for nurturance and sustenance. This groundwork, the substance of our final chapter, relates to children irrespective of genetics or culture.

And it is not children alone who may be kept out of touch with legal and human rights because skin colour has taken precedence over common humanity. Mama (1994) writes of the severity and extent of domestic violence experienced by black women and the time over which they suffer this before seeking to escape. Her research project covered several ethnic communities in the UK which she loosely divided into women of Caribbean, Asian and African origin. Her literature search in respect of women from Africa and the Caribbean discovered none relevant to domestic violence though there were papers on police brutality.

She tells numerous stories of women brutalised by men *whose skin colour was the same as their own*. This was severe, repeated, and suffered in isolation. Mama's stories are of women made homeless by violence, moving from bed and breakfast accommodation to refuges and sometimes back to their abusers. Some accounts are of

avoidance of the police, some of practical help, some of minimisa-
tion of 'domestic incidents' and some, sadly, of racist comments by
police officers.

The strength of Mama's outrage however is directed at the abusing men. She describes husbands or partners who invoke 'tradition'
or 'religion' to justify what they expect in the way of subservient
behaviour from women and children. She points out that none of the
major religious texts condones abuse of women but that men
appropriate these texts in justification of their behaviour. She is concerned also that violence may be accepted by the indigenous country as being part of the black culture and therefore to be condoned
or tolerated.

Many of the women have children. The effects upon them are
indicated; one woman describes her son as frightened, hyperactive,
wetting his bed. She says, 'When we took him to the child psychiatrist, I didn't go in with him and the things he told her – I couldn't
believe it. At the time he was about five – I thought what does he
know about this? He knows everything and it affects him. I cried
when she told me.'

We do have a body of knowledge about the effects upon children
of witnessing interparental violence and this knowledge is not
related to the skin-colour of the people involved. Compared to children from non-violent homes, those who have seen and experienced
violence have more problems with behaviour, especially aggression,
overactivity, rebelliousness and, as they get into adolescence,
becoming delinquent. They are more subject to emotional problems
such as being very unhappy, which may shade into clinical depression and suicide attempts. They show many specific fears and sometimes are obsessional. Children from violent homes show
educational under-achievement and, not surprisingly, are poor at
concentrating on their work and are irregular in attending school.
The social problems include a reduced ability to understand how
other people are feeling or to communicate effectively with them.
Such children are liable passively to withdraw when life doesn't go
as they want it to or to become aggressive (Jaffe et al. 1990, Hotaling
and Sugarman 1989, Jenkins and Smith 1991). Four out of five children who have witnessed acts of violence, even when not injured
themselves (or perhaps even more so when not injured themselves,
since their entire energies may have been focused on what they saw),
show post-traumatic stress disorder and this is more severe and
long-lasting if the violence that the children have seen is caused by
fellow humans, particularly if this has happened within their own
family (Pynoos and Eth 1984, 1986). This, and the interactions
between trauma and grief, are discussed in Chapter 9.

Numerous inquiries about child abuse and neglect have focused on common features such as poor recognition of warning signs and inadequate coordination between services and professionals, as will be discussed in Chapters 9 and 10. At least two inquiries however, those on Jasmine Beckford and Kimberley Carlisle (Blom-Cooper *et al.* 1985, 1987) can, with hindsight, lead to the hypotheses that care-workers, faced with child neglect in a black or a white family, were reluctant actively to intervene even when, as in the case of Jasmine Beckford (who was black), there was evidence of weight loss, failure to attend clinics and an overt leg injury which prevented the child from walking without pain. Non-intervention in the service of 'anti-racism' or 'working with parents' militates against the well-being of women and children who require just the same civil rights as do any other citizens of the state.

Children react differently to violence, in part according to their age and sex. Children in refuges show many health problems and somatic complaints. They tend to be fearful and to act younger than their age. Older children begin to feel considerable guilt, born partly of a conflict of loyalty towards the adults in their lives and partly from supposed responsibility for preventing or averting violence (Layzer *et al.* 1985). Young children can only make sense of what goes on around them from their own perspective, limited because of their youth and inexperience. Research has shown that rows which lead to violence more commonly arise over the care of children than about sex or money (Straus *et al.* 1980), so children can have very direct and immediate reasons for blaming themselves when their mother is attacked although of course they are not responsible for adult violence. Then, boys of violent fathers are particularly vulner-able to problems in developing a male identity, often copying the violence which they have seen in childhood, whereas girls, identify-ing with their mothers as victims, are vulnerable to depression and psychosexual problems (Goldner *et al.* 1990). A common finding, in all domestic injury, is that children know about and can describe violence which neither father nor mother realises that they have seen, as indicated in Mama's interview above (see also Jaffe *et al.* 1990).

Harris Hendriks, Black and Kaplan *et al.* (1993) in their over-view of children who have suffered an extreme form of violence, the death of one parent at the hands of the other, comment that forty per cent of the children whom they have seen are under five years of age at the time of the killing and that, of this group, a substantial minor-ity are pre-verbal or only just able to speak. There is a great deal of work to be done on understanding just what are the effects on such young children. Although there may be variations in how a family deals with violence, according to its ethnic group and cultural back-ground, they would echo Mama's view that the effects upon children should be seen as universal, wrong and to be avoided. These are issues which transcend culture.

There are worse things than being black in a white society. Irrespective of your skin colour, it is worse to be without reliable secure parenting, and worse to be exposed to prolonged or repeated violence within the home and when children are involved in prolonged legal battles in which decision-making about race, culture and identity is allowed to take precedence over basic knowledge about children's needs for safety, nurturance and reliable care.

We are not likely to find out what has happened to Errol. However he was taken from a foster home which would have been willing to care for him long-term. He was placed with a single woman in her fifties who already was responsible for several children older than himself, who lacked a supportive family network such as might have existed in the Caribbean and who, in accepting his care in his second year, commented that she could not have managed him when he was a baby. No account was taken of the effects upon him of traumatic bereavement nor of a necessarily abrupt separation from his foster family who are now two hundred miles away.

For Errol, aftercare was minimal and, since the framework in which it was set up was not one in which his needs had been comprehended, was not likely to identify criteria for deciding whether or not plans were proving to be successful. The overriding criteria indeed were skin colour, blood relationship and (to be cynical) convenience and economy in decision-making.

Jonathan was adopted by his white foster parents. This family, and that of Ronald, may benefit from work such as that of Tizard and Phoenix (1993). They may benefit also from post adoption services but opposition of the respective local authorities to these placements combined with lack of resources may hinder the establishment of this form of help.

Yvonne has a forty per cent lifetime risk of developing a schizophrenic illness (Werry and Taylor 1994). Research on adopted-away children of psychotic parents indicates that the risk is genetic and not simply a matter of environment. It is a matter of good practice rather than research that any child so vulnerable should be offered the best possible help in the way of secure, reliable parenting yet, as with Errol, decisions about race, culture and religion have taken priority over research knowledge and the child's basic needs.

Yvonne is much more in need of parenting, and the cessation of legal battles than she is of knowledge about Trinidad or baptism in a particular faith. Information and knowledge of the effects of racism can be built into her educational experience but she will not be able to make use of any education if she is not nurtured, early and soon.

Ronald did stay in his white foster family. They have sought help from a church with a black pastor in their neighbouring town and, with Ronald's teachers, are exploring how best he may be educated (CRE 1989, Maximé 1987). His grandmother visits regularly and his mother, who has moved to another part of the country, sends cards, photographs and presents.

To sum up, negative discrimination is wrong but as a society we must discriminate, in the original sense of the word, between issues specific to people of particular colour, culture and religion and those common, as basic human rights, to all members of the human race.

8 The legal system: when battles are fought in court

In 1983 Sir Roger Ormrod, a former judge in the Court of Appeal in the United Kingdom, wrote of child care law that it was in a state of confusion unparalled in any other branch of the law now or at any time in the past. Five major statutes were involved, the Children and Young Persons' Act 1969, the Child Care Act 1980, the Guardianship of Minors Act 1971, the Matrimonial Causes Act 1973 and the Adoption Act 1958, as amended by the Children Act 1975.

He added that important parts of the legislation, passed in Parliament, had never been brought into operation.

He described in addition the inherent powers of the High Court, the prerogative powers of the Crown which survive from the past. The King really was *parens patriae*, the father of his people and responsible for all children within his domains. This tradition was outside legislative control, resting with the judges.

The result of this mass of statute law was that every court in the country had some powers over children, but not the same powers, and the Court of Appeal had repeatedly recommended that this chaos was unnecessary, complex and expensive. The aim that the law be reformed from the perspective of the child *vis à vis* the parents and of the parents *vis à vis* the child led to the Children Act 1989 (England and Wales) which was implemented in October 1991. This has attempted to coordinate private law, affecting disputes between individuals, and public law which involves families and children directly with the state. The central aim of this new legislation was that 'the family' should be autonomous and supported. The concept of parental rights was replaced by that of parental responsibility and local authorities were enjoined (though not empowered nor financed) to offer help to 'children in need'. This was meant to be a flexible term covering children with illnesses, children with parents suffering from illnesses or disabilities, children at risk of abuse or neglect and, in theory at least, any child unable, without state intervention, to achieve his or her full potential. Parental responsibility was seen as dwindling as a child grew older until, on reaching adult life, he or she in turn became an autonomous citizen of the state.

Aims of the legislation

The welfare of the child

This rather vague concept is a court's paramount consideration.

1. All proceedings in public and private law are to be established within a timetable which will allow the making of decisions in accordance with the child's needs. Long delays and periods of uncertainty are seen as inherently detrimental to the child's welfare.

2. A checklist is applied in private law proceedings which lead to disputes concerning children (usually in divorce proceedings about where children will live and how often they will see the non-resident parent). The same checklist applies concerning court hearings regarding children who allegedly have been abused or neglected. A court must have regard to:
   (a) the ascertainable wishes and feelings of the child (considered in the light of his or her age and understanding);
   (b) the child's physical, emotional and educational needs;
   (c) the likely effect on the child of any change in circumstances;
   (d) the child's age, sex, background, or any characteristics which the court considers relevant;
   (e) any harm which the child has suffered or is at risk of suffering;
   (f) how capable each of the parents is, and any other person in relation to whom the court considers the question to be relevant, of meeting the child's needs;

(g) the range of powers available to the court in the
proceedings in question.

A fundamental new principle in Section 1(5) is that 'where the court
is considering whether or not to make one or more orders under this
Act with respect to a child, it shall not make the order unless it considers that doing so would be better for the child than making no
order at all'. Thus, rather than making a positive decision that an
order is necessary, the court is required to consider whether non-
intervention in a child's life could remain more effective than active
intervention. As far as possible, a child's circumstances are to be
changed or protected without the use of court orders.

Secondly, when making a care order, that is an order which
empowers the state, via a local authority, to assume parental responsibility, the court must consider as far as reasonably possible, the
plan made by those proposing to look after the child, the child's
wishes and feelings, the views of the parents or any other person who
already has parental responsibility, and also must give due consideration to 'the child's religious persuasion, racial origin and cultural
and linguistic background' (White, Carr and Lowe 1990, Harris
Hendriks and Williams 1992).

Issues of race and culture in the family placement of children

This is the title of a letter from the Chief Inspector of a Social Services Inspectorate W.B. Utting (now Sir William), dated January
1990 and therefore already available when the Children Act (1989)
came into force. It set out the principles which should inform practice in the family placement of children:

Providing child care services in the multi-racial society

Social services must address and seek to meet the needs of children and families from all groups in the community. Society is
made up of people of many different ethnic and racial origins
and of different religious affiliations. The provision of services
which will reach all members of the community calls for the
development within social services departments of awareness,
sensitivity and understanding of the different cultures and
groups in the local community and an understanding of the
effects of racial discrimination on those groups. Necessary
experience and expertise should be provided for in the staffing
of services and through relationships with other professions
and services and with the community. In some areas the local
community may include too great a variety of ethnic groups to

be reflected fully in the composition of staff. In others, departments may be called on only rarely to provide a service for a child or family from a minority ethnic group. In both these circumstances, departments will need to identify sources of advice and help so that the necessary experience, expertise and resources are available when needed. These principles apply to services to help children to remain within their own families as well as to services for children in care and their families, so that children are not admitted to care due to lack of appropriate and effective social work support for the family. This is especially important in the light of indicators that children from certain minority ethnic groups are over-represented in children in care.

In practice this last sentence can be seen as referring in particular to children categorised as 'Afro-Caribbean'. Figures are difficult to obtain, since each social services department keeps its own statistics and since there is still a legacy from the 1970s and early 1980s of reluctance to categorise according to ethnic groups, when it was thought that this act in itself could stigmatise individual children. Subsequently, children with complex ethnic origins have been categorised as 'black', representing a swing of the pendulum from the earlier principle, resulting in oversimplification and rigidity of classification at the other extreme. However, local authorities attempting to provide services for inner city areas containing a multiplicity of ethnic groups have indeed found that children from minority groups, particularly those from the Caribbean, are over-represented within the care system in relation to their numbers within the wider community.

Paragraph 5 of the letter (Utting 1990) continues:

> Where placements are needed or likely to be needed for children from minority ethnic groups or for children of particular religious affiliation, sustained efforts may be needed to recruit a sufficient number and range of foster parents and prospective adopters from those groups and of that religion. Such efforts are essential if all children who need substitute families are to have the opportunity of placement with families who share their ethnic origin and religion.

The letter recommends that local authorities ensure that service resources include arrangements for the recruitment, assessment, approval, preparation and support of a pool of foster parents who may respond to demands on the service. Advice is given but resource issues are not addressed.

Paragraph 6 states:

> In assessing a child's needs social workers should strive for a

real understanding of the child's cultural background and religion and guard against simplistic assumptions of similarity between different ethnic groups. Clients have a right to expect the understanding, knowledge and sensitivity which are essential if their interests are to be served. Assessment must identify and advertisements explain a child's ethnic origins, religion and family experience in such a way as to provide as helpful a guide as possible to the child's needs. Care is needed so that the terms 'black' and 'black family' are not used in isolation in such a way as to obscure characteristics and needs which are of particular importance to groups and to individuals.

The guidelines alert readers that:

> ... prospective carers who could have much to offer a child of minority ethnic origin or of mixed ethnic origin, by virtue of particular knowledge, language, understanding and family or neighbourhood links, may be discouraged from coming forward or be rejected out of hand. A white family which has adopted or is fostering a child of minority ethnic origin or mixed ethnic origin should not be told that the placement of another such child cannot be considered solely on the grounds of general policy. Each case must be considered on its merits, having regard to the needs of children requiring placement.

It may be that the advice concerning 'opportunity of placement with families who share ethnic origin and religion' should contain the qualification 'where appropriate'. It may not be appropriate that rigid requirements by a family of origin, or by social workers, create a situation where a child is given no choice but to live with a family of specific religious beliefs, language or skin colour.

Rigid practice may cause harm. Zeitlin (1993) describes three children with the same mother but different fathers. The eldest, twelve years old, had a black skinned father from the Caribbean whereas the two younger children probably were of Scandinavian descent, with blonde hair and pale skin. All three were in care because of neglect and the local authority, taking literally the injunction that they must consider a child's ethnic origin, wished to split the sisters, placing the eldest with a black family and her sisters separately. The children were extremely indignant at this plan, regarding the links between the three of them as of the utmost importance. Not surprisingly, Zeitlin reports, the eldest child wants to become a lawyer when she grows up.

Andrew

Andrew was three years old when his Scottish mother was killed by his father. The latter had been born in England but of his Trinidad-born parents one was Chinese and the other black skinned, both Muslim in religion.

Andrew did not see the killing and indeed had not been close to his mother, having been brought up in the care of his maternal grandmother. After the killing Andrew was made subject to a care order. The local authority, in weighing up where he should now live, took into account that his grandmother, beside being grief-stricken and full of rage at her daughter's untimely death, was a single parent in poor health. She however strongly claimed that Andrew should stay in the home most familiar to him. He was placed with his father's brother and wife because they were black skinned Muslims and this was thought the most important single decision with regard to the child's future well-being.

The decision was disputed by Andrew's grandmother but by the time it was heard he had already spent the better part of a year with his uncle's family. His father was in prison and the child had not been told the truth about his mother's death, simply that she had died and that his father was working away from home. Andrew became increasingly angry, restless and difficult. By the time he was eight years old he was in temporary foster care, having been given up by his uncle's family who said that they could not cope any longer with his behaviour and yet unable to return to his grandmother to whom he showed his rage and defiance in such a way that she too felt that she could not look after him. He was afraid of behaving like his father, having learned from his grandmother of the crime, but visited his father in prison and expected to live with him on completion of the sentence.

His temporary foster parents were Rastafarians of Jamaican origin whereas his mother had been a Catholic and his uncle's family strict Muslims. Andrew's needs have not been met via racial 'matching'.

We recognise that in writing this book we have instanced examples of practice which has been harmful or disturbing to individual children, and our stories, which, as we indicated in the introduction, have been carefully put together so as to identify no single child, may be matched by many stories of successful same-race, same-culture placements. Our aim is not to denigrate work which takes account of a child's heritage but to indicate the dangers of doctrinaire, over-simplistic decision making. We would be concerned, for example if Maria's children, described in Chapter 2, were retained for a long time in temporary insecure care because they could be placed only with a parent or parents who originated in the Irish Republic.

A proposed revision of the law concerning adoption is to complement the Children Act (1989) and to create a clearer role for decision-making which takes account of children's rights and needs. It recommends that children be made parties to adoption proceedings with the right to legal representation and in general that they should have the services of guardians ad litem (specialist social workers who represent children's interests during a court hearing and who are empowered to instruct solicitors).

The aim is that children will not lose touch with their origins. Direct contact with birth parents will be allowed provided there is agreement to this plan both by the child, according to his age and understanding, and the adoptive parents (though the views of adoptive parents will carry greater weight should they oppose such a plan, since the aim still will be that children are parented by people who feel secure about their role). The current principle, that children should be aware of their adoptive status, will be enshrined in law and they will have rights, at an appropriate age, for access to information on file. (These principles and rights are equally relevant in long-term foster care or placement within extended families.) It is suggested that adoptive parents should be provided with a packet of information to be retained on behalf of the child until his or her eighteenth birthday.

With regard to religion it is proposed that the views of the child in addition to those of his parents should be considered by adoption agencies (a highly relevant consideration in both adoption and child care practice, for example, when one considers the experiences of Andrew described above). There will be greater opportunity for both parents to give their views concerning the choice of prospective adopters. It is made very clear that due consideration must be given to the race, culture and language of the child along the lines of the Children Act, but that in placing a boy or girl in a permanent home 'these issues should not necessarily be more influential than any others'. This should militate against the making of decisions such as that concerning the girl who was expected to leave her half-sisters and move to a home with at least one black parent.

The law will prefer placement of children with married couples or single people but is flexible, considering that careful matching of parent and child is more important than ideology. This may be of particular value where parenting is the responsibility of complex family networks. The guidelines also emphasise that adoption agencies should be flexible in their approach to the age of prospective adopters. This seems highly relevant in child care work since it is very common that children, like Andrew, in part are brought up by members of an earlier generation, or, like Errol, are placed with them. It is a curious anomaly that prospective adopters are currently rigidly assessed regarding age, health, appropriate ethnicity and a host of other factors yet, within the framework of the Children Act (1989), described in Chapter 2, where the priority if possible is that children remain within their families of origin, extremely flexible and sometimes unrealistic assessments have been made. Some grandparents, for example, can do an excellent job, others are full of grief, anger and guilt that their parenting of their own children has been less than successful and are ill-equipped to cope well with the off-spring of disturbed parent-child relationships in the earlier generation. We do not know, for example, whether Andrew's grandmother who had cared for him by default (Brinich 1989) could have coped with Andrew, despite her grief and rage about his mother's untimely death, had she not been prevented for ideological reasons until such time as the child's disturbance and alienation from her precluded his return.

Young offenders

Andrew is likely, as he grows older, to fall foul of the law, as did Vincent (Chapter 5). If black or mixed race young men continue to come before British courts in greater numbers than would be expected from their incidence in the population, they will be at risk from shortsighted current plans for young offenders. For example, there are under 300 places at present where young people under the age of sixteen may be locked up in secure accommodation. It is proposed that a secure training order for 'persistent young offenders' between twelve and fourteen will create demand for 200 more such places and these may be run by the voluntary or private sector as well as by local authorities, which may lead to yet greater provision of lock ups. It is also proposed that the current maximum one year sentence in young offender institutions will be doubled. Vincent, Andrew and other children like them will be particularly at risk of moving from insecure care plans to the juvenile justice system where the 'security' will be a matter of locks and keys.

It is to be hoped that the principles for practice outlined in our final chapter will be applied to all children within our society, irrespective of race, creed or colour and will reduce the risks of such waste and loss to individual families and the society in which they live.

9   It is almost the year 2000

(title of poem by Robert Frost 1966)

What do we know of children's needs?

We know far more about the needs of all children for reliable attachments, nurturance, warmth, socialisation and education, and the effects upon them of bereavement, other losses, dislocation and trauma, than we do about variations related to language or cultural differences. Indeed, many standard and accessible texts (e.g. Bowlby 1969, 1972, 1988, Herman 1992, Parkes *et al.* 1991, Raphael 1982, 1984, Rutter 1981, Rutter and Madge 1976, Rutter and Rutter 1992) provide an introduction and overview of themes crucial to the wellbeing of all our children.

Attachment and the growth of social relationships

Psychoanalytic theory told us that attachments are learned through the feeding process. We now know that this is wrong. Bowlby (1969), Parkes and Stevenson-Hinde (1982), Hinde and Stevenson-Hinde (1988) and Parkes *et al.* (1991) have taught us that attachment behaviour is innate to humans and also can be studied ethologically, for example by observing monkeys and other primates through successive life cycles. It is part of our nature to become social beings;

babies are comforted by social contact and it is in this context that we begin to learn what it is to be human. Very young babies prefer faces to other objects around them and by six weeks old look directly towards those who speak with them. Audio-visual recording of mothers and babies has shown, in great beauty, their mutual dance and the immediate disappearance of this interactive rhythm when a parent is distracted or disturbed.

By three months old babies show preference for the people, most often their mother or father, who take regular care of them and they respond in a more lively way to an expressive face, with laughing, smiling, talking and singing, than to one which is expressionless. Babies respond best to sounds within the range of human speech and skilled parents time their responses to fit in with their baby's smiles and babbling.

By six to eight months old the babies can protest at an unfamiliar caretaker, showing their preference and will turn, even before they can physically move, towards the preferred person, leaning, calling and raising their arms, when they are frightened, in a strange situation or upset.

A wariness of strangers appears; a mother who has been used to keeping an eye on her baby while she walks towards a shop counter one day discovers that this is not enough, the baby also wants to be able to keep an eye on her and will protest vigorously if she moves out of his sight. However, small children are not afraid of strangers provided they are secure with a parent, the approach is gentle and the parent gives signals that the situation is safe and approved. Children of between seven and nine months and upwards will however become very frightened if suddenly picked up by a stranger or removed from the presence of the parent.

These changes protect the baby by alerting his caretakers to danger as does the subsequent use of the toddler, at eighteen months or so, of a parent or caretaker as a secure base from which to explore the world (Ainsworth *et al.* 1978, Bowlby 1988). A securely-based child gradually develops a hierarchy of attachments with parents providing the basis for a pyramid on which are built attachments to siblings, wider family and, later, school and other friendships. The securely-based child shows *attachment behaviour* which develops into *attachments*, some at least of which will be lifelong, leading to the mature interdependence of loving adult human beings who in turn have a capacity to form new attachments, which are sustaining, satisfying and mutually beneficial within the framework of adult life.

Disorders of attachment occur, as indicated in the chapter on fostering and adoption, when opportunities to live in this peaceful, progressive, mutually loving system of relationships are lacking, being either lost, dislocated or disrupted.

Anxiously attached children have difficulty in exploring the world, lacking the secure base from which they may do so. They show prolonged episodes of attachment behaviour which become inappropriate to their age and surroundings, for example refusing at ten years old to leave home for school or insisting on sleeping in a parent's bed. An adolescent may lack social skills, clinging inappropriately to home, parental company and supervision.

Avoidantly attached children also are anxious at separation but, when reunited, continue to protest angrily. They show ambivalence, seeking comfort from their caretaker and then angrily rejecting it. A child of six years old, reunited with her mother after a frightening operation requiring general anaesthesia, hugged her mother while leaning away from her, avoiding eye contact and kicking angrily.

Insecure attachment, the unattached child. These are the most disturbing children. At the extreme are those who, like the Miller of Dee in the rhyme, 'Care for nobody, no not I, And nobody cares for me'. Such children, at a young age, are difficult to care for. A foster parent in charge of an unattached three year old has to watch the child very closely in shops or public places. Of course, all parents would supervise a child of this age but, when the child is unattached, there is no reciprocity, the child does not keep an eye on the parent and make sure that the caretaker stays in sight, but wanders off, putting himself at risk.

Many children who have been abused and neglected show *disorganised attachment*; for example, a child may show attachment behaviour to the parent who has abused or neglected him, confusing inexperienced workers who assume that what looks an obviously non-accidental injury cannot really be so, since the child still clings affectionately to the parent who, on clinical evidence, caused the injury. It is likely that this disorganised attachment, a mixture of clinging, anger, detachment and avoidance, which appear unpredictably and inconsequentially, represent the results of unpredictable and unreliable behaviour by caregivers. The child may be afraid of the person who provides care but at other times acts parentally, being afraid for that person, attempting to protect and to be compliant (Zeanah and Emde 1994, review research in this field). These findings link with what is now known about the effects of violence upon children described in Chapter 7.

Children and grief

Grief occurs when a parent dies, but also when the loss is through illness, or dislocation as when Marsha and her brother (Chapter 5) were sent from what they had experienced as a secure base with their grandmother to the London of the 1960s. Grief and loss can occur also when a parent is too ill to care for a child or is lost because of a court order subsequent to abuse or neglect. In these latter cases, however, grief is complicated by trauma.

The processes of grief in childhood

These have been reviewed by Pynoos (1992) and Black (1993a, 1993b). When it comes to death children can understand more than most adults give them credit for. By five years old the majority know that death is irreversible, happens to everyone, has a cause, means that the lost one is gone forever and that dead people are different from those who live. Children can understand that the dead cannot move, cannot feel, cannot hear, see, smell or speak, that they do not require meat or drink and that they do not perform the other bodily functions with which small children are familiar. The concept of decay and dissolution is harder for young children and most do not grasp this until they are older (Lansdown and Benjamin 1985).

Children not yet able to speak tend to respond to loss with their bodies, those who had become continent may become wet or soil and many show sleep disturbances, or are restless with poor appetite. Children who have been secure show some of the attachment disturbances described above. They are more liable to infections and other illnesses after a loss (Raphael 1982). They can deceive adults about the effects upon them of loss since children, particularly pre-adolescents, tend not to sustain their sad emotions over long periods, nor do they connect their bad behaviour and upset with its cause in a way that can be explained to others. They may attempt to deal with their grief by repetitive play which can be distressing to adults and often a conspiracy of silence develops in which the grown-ups do not speak to the children of their loss, wishing not to disturb them further and the children, dependent on whatever care is still available, do not disturb the parent. Children may hide their own grief in order to protect the surviving parent and because of their extreme need for continuing care.

Reactions to loss appear to be universal, although grief may be expressed in different ways according to cultural and religious practice, the feelings undergone and the process of grief are the same. Moreover, children who have been bereaved show higher levels of emotional disturbance and symptoms for up to two years and, if they lose a parent in childhood, are at increased risk of depression in adult life (see Black 1978 and Goodyer 1990 for an overview of these issues). Children's response to grief also depends on the coping strategies of survivors, a child's suffering may be prolonged or distorted where remaining caretakers are overcome with grief or struggling to avoid it. Under such circumstances, children may suppose that they are to blame for the changed events and feelings around them. New caretakers ('parents by default') who unexpectedly take on responsibility for a bereaved and traumatised child, struggle with complex desires to protect and yet subtly to reject the subjects of their new responsibilities (Brinich 1989).

Children and trauma

How much more do they feel this when events, from the child's point of view and often that of the adults too, are sudden, unexpected, frightening or dangerous. Yet until as recently as 1985 there was considerable doubt within the field of psychiatry and psychology as to whether children reacted even to severe stress other than with mild and temporary changes in emotion and behaviour. This may be because the effects of traumatic stress were studied in adult populations and in the face of extreme situations; the effects of war upon soldiers were studied extensively from the nineteenth century onwards though, as Herman (1992) points out, this knowledge tended to be lost or devalued between wars. Other research has explored the effects upon populations of major disasters and, inasmuch as children have been studied, this has been indirectly through interviews with parents, other caretakers and teachers.

The story changed once direct work began with child survivors. Post-traumatic stress disorder (PTSD) in children has now been studied in relation to violence (e.g. Pynoos and Eth 1985, 1986, Pynoos et al. 1987), kidnapping (Terr 1992), transport disasters (Yule and Udwin 1991, Parry-Jones 1991, 1992), homicide (Harris Hendriks et al. 1993). Black et al. (1995) offer the first English textbook on the effects of psychological trauma in childhood and adult life.

What we now know is that children who experience actual violence or neglect or whose caretaking, familiar routines and surroundings and life patterns are disrupted, even for benevolent or well-intentioned reasons, may show the full range of symptoms recognised and classified in response to studies of major disaster or warfare. For the child, the source of the disaster and dislocation is not the issue: if life is disrupted in a terrifying and unpredictable way, the results will be profound. Of course, if a whole neighbourhood or community is disturbed, as in war, terrorism or disaster, all the adults are affected along with the children and the cataclysm is the greater but, if their caretakers go from the scene, young children, in their disturbance, do not immediately distinguish the greater trouble from the smaller.

Post-traumatic Stress Disorder in Childhood

This can be diagnosed, just as in adults, if a range of symptoms related to a particular stressful event come together in a particular way and last for longer than one month. The American Diagnostic and Statistical Manual (1987 revised) categorises the disorder as follows:

1. Existence of a recognised stressor that would evoke significant symptoms of stress in almost anyone.
2. Re-experiencing of the trauma as evidenced by at least one of the following:
   (a) recurrent and intrusive recollections of the event;
   (b) recurrent dreams of the event;
   (c) suddenly acting or feeling as if the traumatic event were recurring because of an association with an environmental or an ideational stimulus (by this is meant that a sufferer suddenly sees, hears or smells or touches something which triggers a re-experiencing of the trauma);
3. Numbing of responsiveness to or reduced involvement with the external world, beginning some time after the trauma, was shown by at least one of the following: markedly diminished interest in one or more significant activities, feelings of detachment or estrangement from others, constricted affect.
4. At least two of the following symptoms which were not present before the trauma: hyper-alertness or exaggerated startle response, sleep disturbance, guilt about surviving when others have not or about behaviour required for survival, memory impairment or trouble concentrating, avoidance of activities which arouse recollection of the traumatic event, intensification of symptoms by exposure to events that symbolise or resemble the traumatic event.

(American Psychiatric Association 1987)

Children with PTSD try to avoid memories or reminders of the frightening event and this hinders them if they also need to grieve since grieving requires that the child should bring into his mind an image of the lost person or the lost lifestyle. Marsha, bewildered by the impact of London life with a mother she did not remember, was unable to recollect her way of life or family routines in Jamaica, nor could she call to mind the image of her grandmother, who was as lost to her as if death had occurred. If, on the other hand, the most recent memory of the lost person is a very frightening one, a parent bleeding in a car crash, an enraged father striking out, the child will try to put this out of his mind and again the process of grieving is hindered.

It was not realised until direct interviewing, drawing and play with children became the norm, that young ones, like adults, recurrently dream of traumatic events. Flashbacks occur in waking hours, often at times of quiet such as before going to sleep and, for both these reasons, sleeping may be feared and avoided. Flashbacks and intense re-experiencing also occur at quiet times in school and a traumatised child may get an unjust reputation for inattention and forgetfulness. Children in care, whose lives have been dislocated in a traumatic way, are particularly liable to unrecognised PTSD (Harris Hendriks 1989).

The symptoms of PTSD fall into two groups. On the one hand, there is intense arousal with fast-beating heart, sweating, disturbances of digestion and bowel function, and often an intense startle response.

Jennifer, who had seen her mother stabbed to death, would jerk convulsively (her grandmother thought that she was having fits) whenever sudden noises occurred and, in particular, when a police car or ambulance went by with flashing lights. She was two when she lost her mother and these symptoms still persisted when Jennifer was seven years old. William, aged eighteen months, woke from sleep with the startle response of a recently born baby. His eldest sister had been strangled in the bedroom which she had shared with her younger brother. Marsha, used to the quiet of village life broken in the main by animal sounds or human voices, recurrently startled at traffic, car horns and sirens.

Allied with this intense alertness, paradoxically, are feelings of numbness and detachment. Children may deceive the adults around by speaking of what they have undergone in detached, calm voices as though they were unaffected or had recovered. They may be excessively compliant with the adults who care for them and since numb, compliant children may be easier to look after for adults who themselves are traumatised, this may continue because this, the state of affairs unrecognised as being harmful, makes life easier in the short term.

Janice, aged fourteen, had been fostered by a couple who matched, one white skinned and English, the other English-

Jamaican. She was compliant and fitted easily with home routine but gave away little about how she felt. Only after some months in her new home, and with help from a clinical psychologist, was Janice able to speak, not only of the rape which had occurred when she was twelve years old but of her fears of going to sleep, since intense re-experiencing of her attack took place between sleep and waking. This also happened sometimes when she was in class and was so vivid that Janice had secretly worried, for many months, that perhaps she was going crazy (she was frightened that she might become schizophrenic, an example of the layman's use of a frightening word which has led Clare (1994) to the proposition that its use be discontinued). For Janice, healing took time but schoolwork and sleep were improved by explanation and education.

The interaction of trauma and grief

Losses, through death or separation, which occur as a result of traumatic events, usually lead to rapid and numerous changes in a child's life. Under these circumstances a child may lose familiar caretakers, routines, possessions, may be in financial difficulties and usually will be required to change school and often neighbourhood also. For Caribbean immigrants, these changes took place across the Atlantic Ocean. The effects upon the children in turn disturb their new caretakers and cycles of disturbing interaction may follow. Pre-occupied adults, with many other responsibilities, like the London-based parents of Marsha and Greg, will find it difficult to cope with a child's emotional and behavioural baggage.

Children suffer more intensely and persistently when their trouble is caused, or seems to be caused, by adult humans, rather than through natural disaster or catastrophe which no-one could have avoided. For the children of the diaspora, this inevitably was the case and children growing up within UK society have been able to see for themselves that poor housing, limited educational opportunity, negative discrimination and racism are created by humans and are not phenomena of the natural world.

Trauma nightmares, besides being frightening and disturbing in themselves, hinder the possibility of grief dreams which, though painful, create a calmer environment in which there can be comfort and sustenance in the sense of loss. The child who feels numb and constricted in the face of loss again is hindered in grieving since grief requires recollection again and again until this is achieved in a spirit of tranquillity. The hyper-arousal and alertness of trauma often create a pervasive and persistent state of anxiety which makes it hard for children to focus on grieving. All of these problems limit the establishment or maintenance of attachment. If a child has lost those who cared for him or her, the most urgent need, for the many years until independence or mature dependence become realistic possibilities, is for an adult to provide nurturance, love and trust. Yet, all the experiences through which the child has gone limit the establishment of trust even when new reliable care is available. School-work suffers and achievement is undervalued by dispirited carers and by the child (Jackson 1987).

Traumatised children, who have lost what is familiar to them, tend to develop the distorted attachments described earlier, disorganised, discontinuous attachment behaviour being a common result and one particularly problematic for those who wish to help the child to heal. Worst of all perhaps are the non-attached children who behave as though it is never going to be possible to trust again and who try, with disastrous results, to take care of themselves.

Conclusion

This range of knowledge, about attachment, bereavement, loss and trauma has been constructed, and continues to develop, on the basis that all growing children have needs in common. It is a body of knowledge more solid and durable than any yet available about cultural differences between children. When it comes to helping them deal with the major events of life, skin colour is not the primary consideration.

This is not to say of course that cultural differences should not be taken into account when offering mourning rituals and helping a child to recover from trauma. Mulrain (1993), in considering the training of grief counsellors, comments that in all races and cultures the same process of shock, sorrow, anger, guilt, acceptance and resolution takes place. What varies is the way the family and community progress along the painful road trodden in common by all humans who experience loss. Laungani (1994) makes the same point.

Mulrain comments that anthropologists find that personal and public mourning may be distinctive in varying social settings. In some communities bereaved women are expected to declare their sorrow, giving as examples the dramatic expression of Puerto Rican women, the traditional expectation that Greek and Portuguese women will, as might have happened in nineteenth century England, wear mourning clothes and remain faithful always to the dead, is contrasted, by Mulrain, with middle-class American tendencies to regard grief as brief, 'to be gotten through as quickly as possible with successful outcome measured in terms of developing new relations and giving up ties to the dead'. (He is perhaps a little cynical here).

There are variations in funeral ceremonies, Hindus, followers of Islam and Judaism all have in common that there are strict rules regarding who may touch the dead body. In the Caribbean it is customary that the dead person is displayed at the funeral so that all may say a personal farewell. There are variations regarding the value of cremation or burial. People from the Caribbean may be of a variety of faiths, or none, and it is of great importance that a wider community should respect and value the ceremonies and traditions of minority groups. Indeed, 'Westerners' may have much to learn; many mourning rituals of Africa, the Caribbean and of Judaism and Islam, provide a rite of passage at least through the early stages of the long road towards acceptance and resolution.

Mulrain writes that as a boy growing up in Trinidad he would know when one of his Indo-Caribbean friends had lost a relative because his head would be clean-shaven and, in the wider community he would observe dwelling houses with curtains removed and pictures and photographs turned to the wall as a symbol of a death within the family. In his community death was not a private affair but something to be shared and understood. Bereavement was not a process to be undergone in silence and alone.

Children should not undergo trauma, bereavement, loss and dislocation in silence. A body of knowledge should be respected and drawn upon, their common humanity and needs respected as should religion, relevant ritual and custom. All members of a community, adult or child, should be regarded as having these same needs and rights, with access to a common core of understanding.

10 How to use what we know and learn more

Remaining free of all intentional injustice, of all mischief ...
                                           Hippocratic Oath

In 1989 the General Assembly of the United Nations accepted a Convention on the Rights of the Child which was signed by in the United Kingdom in January 1992. This provides principles for practice applicable to all children in any society, even though over much of the earth's surface it presents a distant ideal. The 'rights' which are identified by the convention are those of the child, not of parents or other adults. It recognises however that children are human beings within the framework of the United Nations Universal Declaration of Human Rights and international covenants on human rights. It is 'proclaimed and agreed that everyone is entitled to all the rights and freedoms set forth therein, without distinction of any kind, such as race, colour, sex, language, religion, political or other opinion, national or social origin, property, birth or other status'. 'Childhood is entitled to special care and assistance'. Without getting drawn into controversy as to what the word 'family' means, the convention upholds a child's right to grow up harmoniously in a family environment, in an atmosphere of happiness, love and understanding. Special consideration should be given, throughout the world, to children 'living in exceptionally difficult conditions'.

There is perhaps a baseline of knowledge about which there will be little controversy. All small human animals are in need of clean water, food, warmth and protection from danger. If they are ill or injured they need appropriate care and the community, with parents as the first line of defence, should be so organised as to nurture and protect its young.

All children need opportunities to acquire and practice a language, to explore safely and to learn from their environment and to be educated to take part in, and over time to contribute to, the community of which they are members. They should not be assaulted, abused, wrongfully punished or inappropriately imprisoned.

Almost immediately however room for debate, variety and controversy appears. Which language, in a multi-linguistic society, should a child first learn, how much responsibility and at what age may be given to young children. How best and by whom should education be provided? What constitutes unfair or unreasonable punishment? (It is sad that these issues as to how best to punish children come to the forefront so early and in so many societies.) At what age and under what circumstances may young children and young people be held responsible for their own behaviour if they are criminal or for taking decisions on their own behalf, such as for example giving consent to medical treatment, signing a contract or instructing a lawyer? Even in one society, that of the UK, as indicated many times within earlier chapters, there may be prolonged, understandable and, at least sometimes, reasonable debate about the provision of education, health and social services for young people and their families. While living with birth parents and growing up in a stable environment does not protect young people from the effects of this debate (and nor should it, since debate is healthy and societies change and develop) the strongest controversies and some of the most intense feelings relate to the best interests of children who, for whatever reason, become separated from their birth families and require specialist health, educational and social services provision.

The Convention on the Rights of the Child is interesting in this respect. Article 2 states that 'states parties shall respect and ensure the rights of children in the present convention to each child within their jurisdiction without discrimination of any kind, irrespective of the child's or his or her parents' or legal guardians' race, colour, sex, language, religion, political or other opinion, national, ethnic or social origin, property, disability, birth or other status'. This is almost a reprint of the principle for all citizens in the Universal Declaration. Here however, it specifies that these are the rights of children. The second paragraph continues: 'states parties shall take all appropriate measures to ensure that the child is protected against all forms of discrimination or punishment on the basis of the status, activities, expressed opinions, or beliefs of the child's parents, legal guardians or family members'. This article therefore makes clear that, not only are the child's rights the same as those of adults, but that, where there may be conflict between the child's interests and those of the parent, those of the child, if he is to be fully prepared to live an individual life, are to be given first consideration. It is note-worthy that the convention uses the word 'discrimination' to equal 'negative discrimination', a point we have discussed earlier in this work. It is clear in context, where discrimination and punishment are bracketed together, that, although other parts of the article make it clear that children may need special help, discrimination is used as a pejorative term.) As worded, however, the convention recog-nises that there may be a conflict between a child's parents, guardians or family members concerning race, colour, language or politics and that the child's interests must come first.

This, on occasion, can appear to be in direct conflict with UK law and accepted good practice. We think however that this is a mis-conception, and one that is illustrated earlier within our text.

Thus in 1989 in the UK the Children Act, while still holding the rights of the child as paramount, and emphasising parental respon-sibilities as distinct from parental rights, enjoined upon local authorities a duty to work 'in partnership' with parents, legal guardians and other relevant family members. The making of a care order in favour of the state did not remove parental responsibilities which now are shared with a local authority even after a court order other than adoption has been made.

At the same time, good practice enjoined that, where children could not live with the birth family, their wishes and views should be taken into account with particular reference to a child's 'ethnic origin' (and we have seen how difficult a concept that can be), lan-guage and religion. This has meant on occasion that children have not been placed, or placement has been delayed, because of an assumption that an appropriate choice must be parents of a particu-lar religion or skin colour (in practice these are the two issues to which most attention has been paid). The writers have seen some strange decisions in this regard, such as the placement of an English-born half-Jamaican, half-Scottish child with Nigerian foster parents and the insistence that the child of an Irish Protestant and a Caltholic from the Dominican Republic must be placed with a Catholic family of which one parent was born in Trinidad.

We think that, were the Convention is taken seriously, these rigid views would be adhered to with less certainty since Article 2 makes it clear that negative discrimination, that is, the making of unfavourable or less valuable plans on behalf of a child in need, must not occur on the basis of attributes or wishes of the child's parent or legal guardian. Article 6's assertion that 'states parties shall ensure to the maximum extent possible the survival and development of the child' emphasises the duty to facilitate a child's development. Where conflict or rigid planning or prejudice may hinder a child's development, this should be recognised and avoided.

Article 8 which requires that states parties 'undertake to respect the right of the child to preserve his or her identity, including nationality, name and family relations as recognised by law without unlawful interference' is right and appropriate. The issue is that this is the child's right, not an obligation to be imposed upon him or her by law or by parent or guardian. Difficulties will continue to arise where children are too young to understand the issues and where their primary needs are for care and nurturance and protection but it is important, however young the child, that conflicts are recognised and resolved in terms of the child's rights and needs rather than by legal imposition of adult wishes and belief systems.

Article 5 indicates that the rights and duties of parents and where applicable members of the extended family and community and other legally responsible persons are to provide 'in a manner consistent with the evolving capacities of the child, appropriate direction and guidance in the exercise by the child of the rights recognised in the present convention'. An image from gardening would be of a child being nourished, cherished, protected and facilitated rather than constrained or forced.

Article 4 enjoins that 'states parties shall respect the right of the child to freedom of thought, conscience and religion'. This principle therefore must be balanced alongside the principles in the Universal Declaration of Human Rights and Article 2 which at the same time upholds a child's right to acknowledgment of race, colour, sex, language and religion while enjoining that he not be discriminated against or punished on the basis of the status of his parents and guardians. A child therefore may have the right to be brought up as a member of a Hindu, Muslim, Jewish or Christian community, to be recognised as of a particular ethnic origin (and a child may be both Asian and Muslim or Hindu or Catholic; Haitian and Catholic or free-thinking; Jamaican and Jewish or Baptist) and also must have the right to decide for him or herself about the part that ethnic origins, upbringing and religious belief play upon his role as an adult citizen of the society in which he lives.

The transition between the dependence and receptivity of childhood and the increasing autonomy and responsibilities of adolescence and adult life are problematical in all societies at all times. This book has outlined, and attempted a preliminary discussion of, such conflicts in relation to a minority group of children over a forty year time span but of course they are not unique to time, place or person. The preamble to the Convention considers that 'the child should be fully prepared to live an *individual* life in society and brought up in the spirit of the ideals proclaimed in the charter of the United Nations'. Thus this is the heart of the conflict; the child should grow up to be an individual, autonomous yet part of a community who respect his or her ideals and aims. Yet, along the way, the child may be seen as a possession of that community, with rights indeed, but whose needs far outweigh his rights and whose life must and should be planned in accordance with the wishes, beliefs and language of his family.

In practice, if the conflict is recognised and anomalies in practice debated and dealt with judiciously, equitably and peacefully, all children will do better than when harsh legal conflict, or rigidly defined principles, hinder their slow progress towards maturity. It would be right, for example, that a child brought up by Jehovah's Witnesses should be educated about their beliefs but not that his parents should be enabled to prevent him from having a life-saving blood transfusion. Fortunately extreme examples such as this are rare but the common principle for practice should be that all children are enabled to grow and develop whatever their heritage without constraint or force.

So, what are the principles for good practice concerning children?

The common needs of all children for food, water, warmth, protection and nurturance should be recognised. Each child should be an individual within society, should be prepared to live an individual life and entitled to rights and freedoms irrespective of origins, language, religion or politics. Where there is conflict between the rights of parents and guardians and those of a child, those of the child take precedence.

These principles are the foundations on which a child's life should be built. Next, are the building blocks of knowledge about health, education and social services and the resourcing of a network designed to facilitate service provision. At the top of the pyramid, and least substantial, are blocks of knowledge about the effects of racial and cultural origins on children's health and well-being.

If, when planning for an individual child or a community, we lay our foundations by using the least substantial and secure blocks of knowledge, those about race and culture, the structure that we build is likely to be top heavy and unstable, to the detriment both of the children concerned and of those who build on their behalf. It is essential that we begin on behalf of children with the solid substratum of knowledge concerning their basic needs.

When children are not able to live with their families of origin, the following principles should be sustained (based on the Royal College of Psychiatrists Working Party, Zeitlin *et al.* 1990):

1. Services concerned with planning the assessment, placement, medical treatment and education of children should, as far as possible, be based on research and empirical evidence. This should be supported by clinical practice evaluated by workers in the field and not on political attitudes.

2. Professionals in all services should be chosen first for their skills and education. Specific cultural knowledge, racial background or language skills should be in addition to those required for professional practice and cannot be a substitute for basic knowledge.

3. Specialists in all child services should be offered training which includes an approach to evaluating and understanding the special needs of 'ethnic minority groups'. They should be taught how to analyse issues, to establish research, to study and contribute to the relevant literature. In-service training should be available. Those who do not have specialist knowledge should always be prepared to enlist the help of others who do.

4. Where children are offered education, or specialist services such as psychological treatments, their own self-perception and knowledge of themselves should be taken into account according to their age and understanding.

5. Parents and guardians of children from ethnic minority groups should be helped to educate their children to cope effectively with negative discrimination. Children in turn should be helped to develop a sense of self based on their personal skills and attributes rather than one based on skin colour or identification with a minority group.

6. Where children are offered services relevant to adoption, fostering or other forms of family placement, workers must consider separately the relevance to the mental health and well-being of the children of country of origin, skin colour, 'racial' identification and the child's personal cultural and social experiences.

7. Parents and adoptive parents should be helped openly to discuss with their children social and racial issues, particularly those with special relevance to the children in their care. Wider education on these issues should be available to all parents and all children and their teachers.

8. Where children are unable to live with birth families or may be returned to them after separation, stability and

- quality of parenting and avoidance of long delays and uncertainties should be given high priority. The knowledge we have about attachment theory and about the effects of trauma on children must be applied as appropriate to the age of the child. This knowledge should take priority.

9. Specialist training of social workers, educationists doctors and mental health specialists should include theory and practice relevant to the special problems of minority groups. This should include study of the psychological effects of cultural practice, social stratification, membership of minority groups, identity formation, self-esteem and the effects of social pressure and negative discrimination.

All of these topics, other than that concerning the basic needs of children, are contentious but available for reasoned discussion. This book is but one contribution to a continuing debate and the overall need is for unheated, careful evaluation of current practice, for attempts to identify and integrate what we already know, for recurrent critical review of law and practice, so that patterns do not become entrenched out of custom, without recognition that they may be inappropriate, or that times are changing. And finally, there is need for soundly based and critically evaluated research.

The knowledge that we need, the educational systems that we must develop and the research projects which can be established are not the prerogative of any one ethnic group or profession. We hope that others will criticise our attempts to develop the story of Caribbean children in the United Kingdom and will continue the work to which this is but one small contribution.

List of useful addresses

Afro-Caribbean Mental Health Association, 35–37 Electric Avenue, London SW9 8JP (0171 737 3603).

British Agencies for Adoption and Fostering (for children not able to live with birth families), Skyline House, 200 Union Street, London SE1 9LY (0171 593 2000).

Chidren's Legal Centre, P.O. Box 3314, London N1 2WA (0171 359 9392).

Cruse (Bereavement Care), 126 Sheen Road, Richmond, Surrey TW9 1UR (0181 940 4818).

Family Policy Studies Centre, London NW1 6XE (0171 486 8211).

Family Rights Group, 18 Ashwin Street, London E8 3DL (0171 923 2628).

National Association of Citizens Advice Bureaux, Myddleton House, 115–123 Pentonville Road, London N1 9LZ (0171 833 2181).

National Council of Voluntary Organisations, Regents Wharf, All Saints Street, London N1 9RL (0171 713 6161).

Overseas Adoption Helpline, c/o The Bridge Child Care Consultancy, 34 Upper Street, London N1 0PN (0171 704 2386).

Sickle Cell Society, 54 Station Road, London NW10 4UA (0181 961

7795).

Who Cares (Journal for young people in care), 235–245 Goswell Road, London EC1V 7JD (0171 378 1579).

Young Minds (Mental Health of Children), 22a Boston Place, London NW1 6ER (0171 724 7262).

Youth Access (information and advice for young people), Magazine Business Centre, 11 Newarke Street, Leicester LE1 5SS (01533 558763).

References

Ackroyd, P. (1990) *Dickens* Sinclair Stephenson, London.

Adcock, M. (1993) 'Perspectives on transracial placement' *Association for Child Psychology and Psychiatry Review* 15, 4, 170–172.

Adcock, M., Kaniuk, J. and White, R. (eds) (1993) *Exploring Openness in Adoption* Significant Publications, Croydon.

Ahmad, W.I.U. (ed.) (1993) *'Race' and Health in Contemporary Britain* Open University Press, Buckingham and Bristol.

Ainsworth, M.D., Blehar, M.C., Waters, E. and Wall, S. (1978) *Patterns of Attachment* Erlbaum, Hillsdale, New Jersey.

American Psychiatric Association (1987) *Diagnostical and Statistical Manual of Mental Disorders* 3rd edn, revised. A.P.A., Washington D.C.

Anionwu, E.N. (1993) 'Sickle cell and thalassaemia: community experiences and official response' in *'Race' and Health in Contemporary Britain* Open University, Buckingham and Bristol.

Argent, H. (1987) 'Progress in open adoption' *Adoption and Fostering* 11, 2, 23–24.

Argent, H. (1988) *Keeping the Doors Open: a Review of Post Adoption Services* British Agencies for Adoption and Fostering, London.

Aries, P. (1962) *Centuries of Childhood* Penguin, Harmondsworth, Middlesex.

Bagley, C. and Coard, B. (1975) 'Cultural knowledge and rejection of ethnic identity in West Indian children in London' in *Race and Education across Cultures* Verma, C.K. and Bagley, C. (eds) Heinemann, London.

Bagley, C. and Young, L. (1979) 'The identity, adjustment and achievement of transracially adopted children, a review and empirical report' in Verma, C.K. and Bagley, C. (eds) *Race, Education and Identity* Macmillan, London.

Bakwin, H. (1949) 'Emotional deprivation in infants' *Journal of Paediatrics* 35, 512.

Baldwin, J. (1966) *The Fire Next Time* Michael Joseph, London.

Bebbington, A. and Miles, J. (1989) 'The background of children who enter local authority care' *British Journal of Social Work* **19**, 5, 283–307.

Bender, L. and Yarnell, H. (1941) 'An observation nursery: a study of 250 children in the psychiatric division of Bellevue Hospital' *American Journal of Psychiatry* **97**, 1158–1171.

Benet, M.K. (1976) *The Politics of Adoption* Free Press, New York.

Bennathan, M. (1992) 'The care and education of troubled children' *Young Minds Newsletter* **10**, 1–7.

Bhopal, R. and White, W. (1993) 'Health promotion for ethnic minorities: past, present and future' in *'Race' and Health in Contemporary Britain* Open University Press, Buckingham and Bristol.

Black, D. (1978) 'Annotation: the bereaved child' *Journal of Child Psychology and Psychiatry* **19**, 3, 287–92.

Black, D. (1991) Transracial adoption: applying the literature in child psychiatric practice (unpublished).

Black, D. (1993a) *Children and Bereavement, Highlight 120* National Children's Bureau, London.

Black, D. (1993b) *Traumatic Bereavement in Children, Highlight 121* National Children's Bureau, London.

Black, D., Newman, M., Mezey, G. and Harris Hendriks, J. (eds) (1995) *Psychological Trauma, a Developmental Approach* Gaskell, Royal College of Psychiatrists, London (in the press).

Black, D., Wolkind, S. and Harris Hendriks, J. (eds) (1991) *Child Psychiatry and the Law* Gaskell, Royal College of Psychiatrists, London.

Black, J. (1985), 'Paediatrics among ethnic minorities: Afro-Caribbean and African families', *British Medical Journal* **290**, 984–988.

Blom-Cooper, L., Brown, B., Marshall, P. and Mason, H. (1985) *A Child in Trust* London Borough of Brent.

Blom-Cooper, L., Harding, J. and Milton, E.M. (1987) *A Child in Need* London Borough of Greenwich.

Bohman, M. (1981) 'The interaction of heredity and environment: some adoption studies' *Journal of Child Psychology and Psychiatry* **22**, 195–200.

Bohman, M. and Sigvardsson, S. (1980) 'A prospective longitudinal study of children registered for adoption: a 15-year follow-up' *Acta Psychiatrica Scandinavia* **6**, 339–55.

Bowlby, J. (1969) *Attachment and Loss* vol. 1. Hogarth Press, London.

Bowlby, J. (1972) *Attachment and Loss* vol. 2. Hogarth Press, London.

Bowlby, J. (1980) *Attachment and Loss* vol. 3. Hogarth Press, London.

Bowlby, J. (1988) *A Secure base: Clinical Applications of Attachment Theory* Routledge, London.

Boxall, M. (1976) *The Nurture Group in the Primary School* Inner London Education Authority.

Brinich, P.M. (1989) 'Love and anger in relatives who adopt orphaned children' *Bereavement Care* **8** (2), 14–16.

Bullock, R., Little, M. and Millham, S. (1993) *Going Home: the Return of Children Separated from their Families* Dartmouth, Devon.

Burghes, L. (1994) 'What happens to the children of single parent families?' Editorial *British Medical Journal* **308** 1114–5.

Clare, A. (1994) Stigmatisation in mental illness. Presented at Royal College of Psychiatrists Conference, Cork, Eire.

Clark, K. and Clark, M. (1947) 'Racial identity and preference in Negro Children' *Journal of Social Psychology* SSPI Bulletin 10, 591–9.

Clarke, A.M. (1981) 'Adoption studies and human development' *Adoption and Fostering* **104**, 2, 17–19.

Commission for Racial Equality (1984) *Code of Practice*, CRE, London.

Commission for Racial Equality (1989) *From Cradle to School: a practical guide to race equality and childcare* CRE, London.

Cosman, C., Keefe, J. and Weaver, K. (1978) *The Penguin Book of Women Poets* Penguin, Harmondsworth, Middlesex.

Cullen, D. (1994) 'How amenable are contact disputes to judicial resolution?' *Adoption and Fostering* 18, 1, 31–32.

Davey, A. and Norburn, M. (1980) 'Ethnic awareness and ethnic differentiation amongst primary school children' *New Community* 8, Nos. 1 & 2.

de Mause, L. (1976) *The History of Childhood* Souvenir Press, London.

Department of Health (1994) *Sickle Cell, Thalassaemia and other Haemoglobinopathies* Standing Medical Advisory Committee, HMSO, London.

Dickens, C. (1837) *Oliver Twist* Chapman & Hall, London.

Dickens, C. (1848) *Dombey and Son* Chapman & Hall, London.

Dickens, C. (1853) *Bleak House* Chapman & Hall, London.

Dickens, C. (1854) *Hard Times* Chapman & Hall, London.

Dickens, C. (1865) *Our Mutual Friend* Chapman & Hall, London.

Figueroa, J. J. (1992) *The Chase* Peepal Tree Press, Leeds.

Figueroa, J. J. (1971) (ed.) *Caribbean Voices* George Evans, London; and (1973) Robert B. Luce & Company, Washington/New York.

Figueroa, J. J. (ed.) (1971b) *Society, Schools and Progress in the West Indies* Pergamon, Oxford.

Flaubert, G. (1857) *Madame Bovary* (1981) Bantam Classics, London.

Francis, E. (1994) 'Psychiatric racism and social police: black people and the psychiatric services' in James, W. and Harris, C. (eds) *Inside Babylon* Verso, London & New York.

Fratter, J., Rowe, J., Sapsford, D. and Thoburn, J. (1991) *Permanent Family Placement* Research Series 8, British Agencies for Adoption and Fostering, London.

Frost, R. (1966) *Collected Works* Jonathan Cape, London.

Gill, O. and Jackson, B. (1983) *Adoption and Race: Black, Asian and Mixed Race Children in White Families* Batsford Academic and Educational, London.

Goldner, V., Penn, P., Sheinberg, M. and Walker, G. (1990) 'Love and violence: gender paradoxes in volatile attachments' *Family Process* 29, (4), 343–64.

Goodyer, I.M. (1990) *Life Experiences, Development and Childhood Pathology* John Wiley, New York.

Harris, A. and Hendriks, A.L. (1988) *Check* Headland Press, Merseyside.

Harris Hendriks, J. (1989) 'The health needs of children in care' *Adoption and Fostering* 13, 43–50.

Harris Hendriks, J., Black, D., and Kaplan, T. (1993) *When Father Kills Mother: Guiding Children through Trauma and Grief* Routledge, London.

Harris Hendriks, J. and Black, M. (1990) (eds.) *Child and Adolescent Psychiatry; into the 1990s* Occasional Paper 8, Royal College of Psychiatrists, London.

Harris Hendriks, J. and Williams, R. (1992) 'the Children Act 1989 (England and Wales). Implications for health care practice and schools' *Newsletter of the Association of Child Psychology and Psychiatry* 14, 5, 213–227.

Harrison, G., Owens, D., Holton, A., Neilson, D. and Boot, D. (1988) 'A prospective study of severe mental disorder in Afro-Caribbean patients' *Psychological Medicine* 18, 643–57.

Hendriks, A.L. (1965) *On This Mountain* Deutsch, London.

Hendriks, A.L. (1988) *To Speak Simply* Hippopotamus Press, Somerset.

Hermann, J.L. (1992) *Trauma and Recovery* Basic Books, New York.

Hersov, L. (1990) Aspects of Adoption. The seventh Jack Tizard Memorial Lecture. *Journal of Child Psychology and Psychiatry* 31, 4, 493–510.

Hersov, L. (1994) 'Adoption' in: Rutter, M., Taylor, E. and Hersov, L. (eds) *Child and Adolescent Psychiatry: Modern Approaches*, Blackwell Scientific, Oxford.

Hickling, F.W. (1992) 'Racism: an Afro-Jamaican perspective' *British Medical*

Journal **305**, 1102.

Hinde, R. and Stevenson-Hinde, J. (1988) *Relationships within Families: Mutual Influences* Clarendon Press, Oxford.

Hotaling, G.T. and Sugarman, D.B. (1989) 'Intrafamilial violence and crime and violence outside the family', in Ohlin, L. and Toury, M. (eds) *Family Violence Vol. II, Crime and Justice: a review of research* University of Chicago Press, Chicago.

Howard League for Penal Reform (1993) *The Voice of a Child: the Impact on Children of their Mother's Imprisonment* Howard League, London.

Hyde, H. Montgomery (1976) *Oscar Wilde* Methuen, London.

Ismay, M. (1989) 'Surviving' in Cobham, R. and Collins, M. (eds) *Watchers and Seekers* Women's Press, London.

Jackson, S. (1987) 'The education of children in care' *Bristol Papers on Applied Social Studies* University of Bristol.

Jaffe, P.G., Wolfe, D.A. and Wilson, S.K. (1990) *Children of Battered Women* Sage, Newbury Park.

James, L. (1968) *The Islands in Between: Essays on West Indian Literature* Oxford University Press, London.

James, W. (1994) 'Migration, racism and identity formation: the Caribbean experience in Britain' in James, W. and Harris, C. (eds) *Inside Babylon* Verso, London & New York.

James, W. and Harris, C. (eds) (1994) *Inside Babylon: the Caribbean Diaspora in Britain* Verso, London & New York.

Jenkins, J.M. and Smith, M.A. (1991) 'Factors affecting children living in disharmonious homes: maternal reports' *Journal of the American Academy of Child and Adolescent Psychiatry* **29**, 160–8.

Kadushin, A. (1970) 'Single parent adoptions: an overview and some relevant research' *Social Sevices Review* **44**, 263–274.

Kingsley, C. (1863) *The Water Babies* now published by Blackie and Son, London.

Lamming, G. (1953) *In the Castle of My Skin* Michael Joseph, London.

Lansdown, R. and Benjamin, G. (1985) 'The development of the concept of death in children aged 5–9 years' *Childcare, Health and Development* **11**, 1, 13–20.

Lau, A. (1993) 'Report of North East Thames Child and Adolescent Psychiatrists Working Party on transracial adoption' *Review of the Association for Child Psychology and Psychiatry* **15**, 4, 165–169.

Laungani, P. (1994) Patterns of bereavement in Indian and English Society. Presented at 4th International Conference on Grief and Bereavement. Stockholm.

Layzer, J.I., Goodson, B.D. and Delange, C. (1985) 'Children in shelters' *Response* **9**, 2, 2–5.

Littlewood, R. (1986) 'Ethnic minorities and the Mental Health Act: patterns of explanation' *Bulletin of the Royal College of Psychiatrists* **10**, 306–8.

Littlewood, R. and Cross, S.S. (1980) 'Ethnic minorities and psychiatric services' *Sociology of Health and Illness* **2**, 194–201.

Littlewood, R. and Lipsedge, M. (1981) 'Some social and phenomenological characteristics of psychotic immigrants' *Psychological Medicine* **11**, 303–18.

Littlewood, R. and Lipsedge, M. (1988) 'Psychiatric illness among British Afro-Caribbeans' *British Medical Journal*, **296**, 950–951.

Lobo, E. (1978) Personal Communication.

Macaskill, C. (1985) *Against the Odds: Adopting Mentally Handicapped Older Children* British Agencies for Adoption and Fostering, London.

Malluccio, A.N., Fein, E. and Olmstead, K.A. (1986) *Permanency Planning for Children: Concepts and Methods* Tavistock, London.

Mama, A. (1994) 'Women abuse in London's black communities' in James, W. and Harris, C. (eds) *Inside Babylon: the Caribbean diaspora in Britain* Verso, London & New York.

Manley, M. (1974) *The Politics of Change: A Jamaican Testament* Deutsch, London.

Maximé, J.E. (1987) *Black Identity. Workbook* (Black like me series) Emani Publications, London.

Maximé, J.E. (1993) 'The importance of racial identity for the psychological well-being of black children' *Review of the Association for Child Psychology and Psychiatry* 15, 4, 173–179.

McGovern, D. and Cope, R.V. (1987) 'The compulsory detention of males of different ethnic groups' *British Journal of Psychiatry* 150, 505–12.

Millham, S., Bullock, R., Hosie, K. and Little, M. (1986) *Lost in Care: the Problems of Maintaining Links between Children in Care and their Families* Gower, Aldershot.

Morris, M. (1973) *The Pond* Beacon Books, London.

Mulrain, G. (1993) 'Bereavement, race and culture' *Bereavement Care* 12, 3, 33–35.

Murch, M. and Hooper, D. (1992) *The Family Justice System* Family Law, Bristol.

Naipaul, V.S. (1962) *The Middle Passage* Deutsch, London.

Ormrod, R. (1983) 'Child care law: a personal perspective' *Adoption and Fostering* 7, 4, 10–17.

Parkes, C.M. and Stevenson-Hinde, J. (eds) (1982) *The Place of Attachment in Human Behaviour* Tavistock, London.

Parkes, C.M., Stevenson-Hinde, J. and Marris, P. (eds) (1991) *Attachment across the Life Cycle* Tavistock, Routledge, London.

Parry-Jones, W. (1989) 'Annotation: the history of child and adolescent psychiatry: its present-day relevance' *Journal of Child Psychology and Psychiatry* 30, 1, 3–11.

Parry-Jones, W. (1991) Post-disaster morbidity in children and adolescents (unpublished).

Parry-Jones, W. (1992) 'The impact of disasters on children and adolescents' *Young Minds Newsletter* 10, 10–12.

Parry-Jones, W. (1994) 'History of child and adolescent psychiatry' in Rutter, M., Taylor, E. and Hersov, L. (eds) *Child and Adolescent Psychiatry: Modern Approaches* Blackwell, Oxford.

Pynoos, R.S. (1992) 'Grief and trauma in children and adolescents' *Bereavement Care* 11, 1, 2–10.

Pynoos, R.S. and Eth, S. (1984) 'The child as witness to homicide' *Journal of Social Issues* 40, 87–108.

Pynoos, R.S. and Eth, S. (1985) 'Children traumatised by witnessing acts of personal violence: homicide, rape or suicide behaviour' in Eth, S. and Pynoos, R.S. (eds) *Post-traumatic Stress Disorder in Children* A.P.A., Washington D.C.

Pynoos, R.S. and Eth, S. (1986) 'Witness to violence: the child interview' *Journal of the American Academy of Child and Adolescent Psychiatry* 18, 647–57.

Pynoos, R.S. Frederick, C., Nader, K. and Arroyo, W. (1987) 'Life threat and post traumatic stress in school age children' *Archives of General Psychiatry* 44, 1057–63.

Quinton, D. and Rutter, M. (1988) *Parental Breakdown: the Making and Breaking of Inter-generational Links* Avebury, Aldershot.

Raphael, B. (1982) 'The young child and the death of a parent' in Parkes C.M. and Stevenson-Hinde J. (eds) *The Place of Attachment in Human Behaviour* Tavistock, London.

Raphael, B. (1984) *The Anatomy of Bereavement: a Handbook for the Caring Professions* Hutchinson, London.

Roots Sista, (1987) 'Dictionary Black' in Cobham, R. and Collins, M. (eds) *Watchers and Seekers* Women's Press, London.

Rowe, J., Cain, H., Hundleby, M. and Keane, A. (1984) *Long Term Foster Care* Batsford, London.

Rowe, J., Hundleby, M. and Garnett, L. (1989) *Child Care Now. Research Series 6.* British Agencies for Adoption and Fostering, London.

Rutter, M. (1981) *Maternal Deprivation reassessed* 2nd edn. Penguin Books, Harmondsworth, Middlesex.

Rutter, M. and Madge, M. (1976) (eds) *Cycles of Disadvantage, a Review of the*

Research Heinemann, London.

Rutter, M. and Rutter, M. (1992) *Developing Minds: Challenge and Continuity across the Lifespan* Penguin, Harmondsworth, Middlesex.

Rwegellera, G.G.C. (1977) 'Psychiatric morbidity among West Africans and West Indians living in London' *Psychological Medicine* 7, 317–29.

Sashidharan, S.P. and Francis E. (1993) 'Epidemiology, ethnicity and schizophrenia' in Ahmad, W.I.U. (ed) *'Race' and Health Contemporary Britain* Open University Press, Buckingham and Bristol.

Senior, A. and Bhopal, R. (1994) 'Ethnicity as a variable in epidemiological research' *British Medical Journal* 309, 327–330.

Spencer, J.R. and Flin, R. (1993) (2nd edn) *The Evidence of Children: the Law and the Psychology* Blackstone Press, London.

Stewart, G. and Tutt, N. (1987) *Children in Custody* Avebury, Aldershot.

Straus, M., Gelles, R. and Steinmetz, S. (1980) *Behind Closed Doors: Violence in the American Family* Anchor Press, Doubleday, New York.

Terr, L.C. (1992) *Too Scared to Cry* Basic Books, New York.

Thoburn, J. (1988) *Child Placement: Principles and Practice* Community Care Practice Handbooks, Wildwood House, Aldershot.

Thoburn, J. (1989) *Success and Failure in Child Placement* Gower, Aldershot.

Thompson, F. (1945) *Lark Rise to Candleford* Oxford University Press.

Tizard, B. (1977) *Adoption: A Second Chance* Open Books, London.

Tizard, B. (1991) 'Intercountry adoption: a review of the evidence' *Journal of Child Psychology and Psychiatry* 32, 5, 743–756.

Tizard, B. and Phoenix, A. (1989) 'Black identity and trans-racial adoption' *New Community* 15, 427–437.

Tizard, B. and Phoenix, A. (1993) *Black, White or Mixed Race: Race and Racism in the Lives of Young People of Mixed Parentage* Routledge, London.

Triseloitis, J. (1983a) 'Identity and security in adoption and long-term fostering' *Adoption and Fostering* 7, 22–31.

Triseliotis, J. (1983b) *In Search of Origins; the Experiences of Adopted People* Routledge and Kegan Paul, London.

Triseliotis, J. (1984) *Hard to Place: the Outcome of Late Adoptions and Residential Care* Heinemann, London.

Triseliotis, J. (1989) 'Foster care outcome: a review of key research findings' *Adoption and Fostering* 12, 1, 5–17.

United Nations General Assembly (1989) *Convention on the Rights of the Child* (1992) HMSO, London.

Utting, W. (1990) Issues of Race and Culture in the Family Placement of Children. Letter to Directors of Social Services, Department of Health, London.

Van Keppel, M. (1991) 'Openness in adoption: birth parents and negotiated adoption agreements' *Adoption and Fostering* 15, 4, 81–90.

Vertovec, S. (1994) 'Indo–Caribbean experience in Britain' in James, W. and Harris C.. (eds) *Inside Babylon* Verso, London & New York.

Walcott, D. (1990) *Omeros* Harper Collins, New York.

Werry, J.S. and Taylor, E. (1994) 'Schizophrenia' in Rutter, M., Taylor, E. and Hersov, L. (eds) *Child and Adolescent Psychiatry: Modern Approaches* Blackwell Scientific, Oxford.

Williams, E. (1955) *My Relations with the Caribbean Commission 1943–1955* Port of Spain, Trinidad.

Wilson, A. (1987) *Mixed Race Children: a Study of Identity* Allen and Unwin, London.

White, R., Carr, P. and Lowe, N. (1990) *A Guide to the Children Act (1989)* Butterworth, London.

Wolff, S. (1987) Prediction in child care' *Adoption and Fostering* 11, 1, 11–17.

Wolkind, S. (ed.) (1979) *Medical Aspects of Adoption and Foster Care* Spastics

International, Heinemann, London.

Wolkind, S. and Kozaruk, A. (1983) 'The adoption of children with medical handicap' *Adoption and Fostering* 7, 1, 32–35.

Wolkind, S. and Rushton, A. (1994) 'Residential and foster family care' in Rutter, M., Taylor, E. and Hersov, L. (eds) *Child and Adolescent Psychiatry: Modern Approaches* Blackwell Scientific, Oxford.

World Health Organisation (1988) *International Statistical Classification of Diseases, Injuries and Causes of Death (ICD10)* WHO Geneva.

York-Moore, D. (1994) 'Parental guilt and respite care' *British Medical Journal* 308, 1244.

Yule, W. and Udwin, O. (1991) 'Screening child survivors for post traumatic stress disorders – experiences from the Jupiter sinking' *British Journal of Psychology* 30, 131–8.

Zeanah, C.H. and Emde, R.N. (1994) 'Attachment disorders in infancy and childhood', in Rutter, M., Taylor, E. and Hersov, L. (eds) *Child and Adolescent Psychiatry: Modern Approaches* Blackwell Scientific, Oxford.

Zeitlin, H. (1993) 'Children put love first, not black or white' *The Independent Newspaper* 12 July 1993.

Zeitlin, H., Harris Hendriks, J., Sein, E., Garralda, E. and Cassel, D. (1990) *Child Psychiatry in a Multi-Ethnic Society* Report for Child and Adolescent Psychiatry Specialist Section: Royal College of Psychiatrists, London.

Index